The Animal That Never Was

Lumen Books
446 West 20 Street
New York, NY 10011
(212) 989-7944

© 1992 Lumen, Inc.
ISBN 0-930829-20-4
Printed in the Unites States of America

Lumen Books are produced by Lumen, Inc., a tax-exempt, non-profit organization. This publication is made possible, in part, with public funds from the New York State Council on the Arts, the National Endowment for the Arts, and private contributions.

THE ANIMAL THAT NEVER WAS
(In Search of the Unicorn)

Matti Megged

Lumen Books

Contents

Acknowledgments

I am most grateful to Paul Rotterdam, whose drawings of the Unicorn initiated me into the search for this mysterious animal.

I am in great debt to five scholars, whose books have guided me in my work and led me to the literature about the Unicorn: Odell Shepard, *The Lore of the Unicorn*; Jürgen Werinhard Einhorn, *Spiritalis Unicornis: Das Einhorn als Bedeutungsträger in Literatur und Kunst des Mittelalters*; Rüdiger Robert Beer, *Unicorn, Myth and Reality*; Richard Ettinghausen, *The Unicorn: Studies in Muslim Iconography*; Margaret Freeman, *The Unicorn Tapestries*.

Carlotta Raum, Meg and Fred Licht, and Luigi Sansone helped me to find paintings and reliefs of the Unicorn in Germany and Italy, and I'm grateful to them, as well as to my wife Dore Ashton, who was my companion and quite often my guide in the search.

Many others have helped to find the Unicorn in art and books, and I'm grateful to all of them.

Special thanks to Ronald Christ, who devoted time, insight, and energy to editing my book.

M.M.

Illustrations

Paul Rotterdam, *The Unicorn* (drawing, courtesy of the artist, New York)

Prologue
The Creature That Does Not Exist

One day, in 1985, I happened to visit an art gallery in Boston and saw there a series of drawings by Paul Rotterdam, titled "The Unicorn."

I had seen the Unicorn before, and admired his beautiful image in the tapestries at the Musée Cluny, Paris, and at the Cloisters, New York, and probably in some other places. But I admit I had never paid any particular attention to that creature and had never thought I would.

I was moved by Paul Rotterdam's drawings in spite of, or because of, the fact that the Unicorn himself did not exist in them. Or, rather, did not appear, but was hidden behind a dense texture of graphite lines on paper, hovering around or above an empty space. The physicality of the dense lines was certainly charged by associations with nature—fences of trees and bushes. But my interest was focused on the empty spaces, surrounded by the fence-like structure. What was alluded to there, in those visionary islands of void?

Paul Rotterdam had named his drawings "The Unicorn." But where was he (or she, or it)? Did the interplay between the graphite lines and the void allude to some mysterious hiding place, the enclosed garden of the Unicorn?

Looking at these drawings I recalled one of Rilke's *Sonnets to Orpheus*:

> *Oh, this is the animal that doesn't exist.*
> *They didn't know that, and in any case—*
> *its neck, its bearing, its stride,*
> *and the light of its calm gaze—they have loved.*
>
> *In fact, it never was. But since they loved it,*
> *a pure animal came to be. They always left*
> *enough space.*
> *And in that space, clear and unlocked,*
> *it freely raised its head and did not*

1

need to be. They nourished him not with grain,
but always with the possibility to be.
And they gave the animal such a power

That from its forehead a horn grew. One horn.
To a maiden he came thereby, all white—
and was inside the mirror-silver, and in her.[1]

"They," in Rilke's sonnet, are the poets and the artists who for many epochs and in different cultures have recreated the Unicorn, nourished it with the power to be, caused him to exist. But, in Rilke's sonnet, as well as in Rotterdam's drawings, the Unicorn remains hidden, unknown, an enigma. The drawings and the sonnet initiated me, and the enigma became a challenge. I then started my own search for the Unicorn, the creature that never was, yet was so much alive in many hundreds of works of art—paintings, drawings, tapestries, reliefs—and in poems, legends and stories.

The search took me more than three years of looking for the Unicorn, in various books and works of art, from the Jakarta and Mahabharata and the Old Testament to Yeats and Rilke; from early Assyrian and Persian sculptures and engravings to the paintings of Moreau, Böcklin, Chagall and Fuchs; through numberless drawings, tapestries, poems of late medieval times and the Renaissance in Europe. For me it was an adventurous journey, full of surprises and pitfalls, findings and missings. From the reference books I learned how many Unicorns I've missed in my journey and probably will never find. On the other hand, I've often found the Unicorn in places and even in books where I did not expect him.

The first and most obvious finding of my search, common to all the Unicorns I've seen and read about, was that the myths of the Unicorn, their verbal and visual manifestations, are always haunted by a doubting of the Unicorn's existence, by incredulity, by repeated questions about his nature and meaning. From his earliest appearance in poetry and art, the

Unicorn has been a challenge and an enigma. He has always been perceived as an ambiguous creature, who kept revealing himself through hiding. He never lets it be known who he is, where he is, whether he's alive or dead. Of all the mythical creatures I know about, the Unicorn is certainly the most paradoxical. On one hand, he's one of the most popular creatures, one who has never lost his attraction—even in our sophisticated time—and always shows an amazing, almost miraculous capability for perpetual resurrection. On the other hand, he's always followed by the question, how can he exist when all of those who wrote about him or painted him knew or felt that he never really was, or, if he did exist, that he always disappeared in the unknown, unseen void?

From early times, the world was full of mythical creatures. Some of them were real, natural, and acquired mythical character in certain periods, in certain cultures. Some of them were the pure invention of human imagination or need and were never seen in natural life. But all these mythologized creatures, both the biological and the imaginary, were real and alive, undoubtedly, so long as they carried on their functions in the mythical world, in rituals, in folklore. In other words, so long as they belonged to a certain myth, their existence and function were never challenged by doubt.

In contrast to almost all other mythical creatures, the Unicorn has tended to appear and reappear in different periods, different cultures, without carrying any specific and defined purpose or function. He has always been encountered by doubt, if not heresy, and at the same time continued to exist and to attract the creative imagination.

The ancient Chinese, for example, had four intelligent animals: the dragon, the phoenix, the tortoise, and the Ki-lin—the Unicorn.[2] The first two are imaginary. The tortoise is "real," but acquired mythical traits. Each of them always maintained its specific character and functions—a certain routine and regularity. Only the Ki-lin remained an exceptional creature in his behavior and the irregularity of his appearance, or his inclination to disappear. The Ki-lin (or Chi-lin),* we read, was first seen by the Emperor Fu Hsi, c. 2800 B.C.E., standing near the Yellow River: a multicolored animal whose horn was made of silver. From the Ki-lin the Emperor learned the art of writing. For some reason, typical of all the Unicorns, the Ki-lin disappeared for a long period, until he was seen again by the Emperor Huang Ti, c. 2600 B.C.E., before his death. Since then, he has appeared again only infrequently, either to portend happiness and good luck, or, quite often, to foretell bad news, like the death of a ruler or of a great and holy man.

When Kung-Fu-Tse's (Confucius's) mother bore him in her womb, we read that the spirits of five planets brought her an animal having the shape of a cow, the scales of a dragon, and a horn on its forehead. According to another version, the animal appeared on its own and spat out a jade tablet, on which these words were written: "Son of mountain crystal, when the dynasty crumbles, thou shalt rule as a throneless king." Seventy years later, some hunters killed a Ki-lin, who still had a bit of ribbon around his horn that Kung-Fu-Tse's mother had tied there. Kung-Fu-Tse went to look at the Unicorn and wept because he felt what the death of this innocent and mysterious animal foretold, and because in that ribbon lay his past.[3]

Four hundred years after Confucius's death, the Unicorn appeared again, and the Emperor Wo Ti (Han dynasty) built for him a special room in his palace. Both the times and the places of the Ki-lin's appearance continued to be irregular and unexpected, thus differing from the habits or the rites of other divine animals.

In the 9th century C.E., a Chinese poet wrote: "It is universally held that the Unicorn is a supernatur-

*Some scholars suggest that his name is derived from *Chi-lien*, which means heaven.

al being and of auspicious omen; so say the odes, the annals, the biographies of worthies, and other texts whose authority is unimpeachable. Even village women and children know that the Unicorn is a lucky sign." But even according to this writer, the Unicorn remained enigmatic: "It is not always easy to come across, it does not lend itself to zoological classification. Nor is it like the horse or bull, the wolf or deer. In such circumstances we may be face to face with a Unicorn and not know for sure that we are. We know that a certain animal with a name is a horse, and that a certain animal with horns is a bull. We do not know what the Unicorn looks like."[4]

Such words were never applied to another animal, neither to a holy creature nor to a natural one. We know from several Chinese sources that the Ki-lin "is to come in the shape of an incomparable man, a revealer of mysteries, supernatural and divine, and a great lover of all mankind. He is expected to come about the time of a particular constellation in the heavens, on a special mission for their benefit."[5]

Was the Ki-lin, then, an emissary of heaven, "in the shape of man"? According to other sources, the Ki-lin has the body of a stag, the hoofs of a horse, the tail of an ox, and a single horn twelve feet long springing from the middle of his brow. He is resplendent in the five sacred colors that are the symbols of his perfection. Was he then the king of beasts, a horse from heaven? And if so, how could the hunters kill him, as we read in the story about Confucius? The descriptions of the Chinese Ki-lin differ from each other. What is common to all of them is that he never acquired any specific rite. He was always solitary, would not be captured and was rarely seen, and tended to disappear for long periods. His mystery is different from that of any other "heavenly horses" since his mere existence—whether heavenly or earthly—is always haunted by doubts.

When we turn from the Far East to the West, we do find several descriptions of the Unicorn as a "real," natural creature. But, if we read them carefully, we see that they too were tainted by riddles and doubts. The earliest description of the Unicorn known to us is included in *Indica Opera*, written by Ctesias, a Greek physician in the court of Darius II and Ataxerxes, kings of Persia at the end of the 5th century B.C.E.

According to Ctesias, "There are in India certain wild asses which are as large as horses and even larger. Their bodies are white, and their eyes dark blue. They have a horn on the forehead which is about a foot and a half in length. The dust filed from this horn is administered in a potion as a protection against deadly drugs. The base of the horn is pure white, the upper part is sharp and of a vivid crimson; and the remainder, or middle portion, is black. Those who drink out of these horns, made into drinking vessels, are not subject, they say, to convulsions or to the holy disease [epilepsy]. Indeed, they are immune even to poisons."[6]

(Ctesias's remark about the use of the Unicorn's horn played quite an important role in the literature about the Unicorn in the 15th to 17th centuries in Europe. It was, directly or indirectly, connected with other aspects of the Unicorn myth, but I prefer not to deal with the pragmatic side of this myth, although it might help our understanding of the ways in which a myth grows.)

Ctesias was a physician, and he certainly did not intend to write about a mythical animal. He asserted that his book was perfectly true and based either on what he himself had seen or else had heard from credible witnesses. Yet Ctesias himself had never been in India, and even if he believed the stories of these "credible witnesses," the India in his book remained a mysterious, unknown place, full of wonders and astonishing creatures. As a "man of science," Ctesias himself found it necessary to point out that "other asses, both the tame and the wild, and in fact all animals with solid hoofs, are without the ankle-bone and have no gall in the liver. But these [Unicorns] have both the ankle-bone and the gall. This ankle-bone, the most beautiful I have ever seen, is like that of an ox in general appearance and in size, but it is as heavy as lead and its color is that of cinnabar through and through. The animal is exceedingly swift and powerful, so that no creature can overtake it."[7]

Ctesias's book was probably the main source of the later Greek and Roman descriptions of the Unicorn and was mentioned again, in the 15th and 17th centuries, as a reliable authority on this subject. The common element in all these descriptions is the mixture of the intention to write about a "real" animal, existing in nature, and the doubts of the writers themselves whether such an animal could or did exist.

Aristotle, in his *Historia Animalium*, wrote the following description of the Unicorn: "There are some animals that have one horn only, for example the Oryx, whose hoof is cloven, and the Indian ass, whose hoof is solid. These creatures have their horn in the middle of their head." But, according to Aristotle, "We have never seen an animal with a solid hoof and with two horns, and there are only a few that have a solid hoof and one horn. Of all the animals with a solid hoof, the Indian ass alone has a talus."[8] Aristotle, too, was not dealing with mythical creatures. He intended to include the one-horned Indian ass in his prudent categories of all animals. But the one-horned creature did not fit any of these categories and remained exceptional, a topic of wonder and doubt.

This is true about all the descriptions of the Unicorn in Greek and Roman literature. Aelian, in his *De Historia Animalium* (about 170-235 B.C.E.) followed Ctesias and Aristotle, and wrote: "I have found that wild asses as large as horses are to be seen in India. . . . The body . . . has a horn on the brow," etc. As a prudent historian of the *Animalium*, Aelian never said that he had really seen the Unicorn. He always added the careful warning: "They say. . . . " *They*, whoever they were, say, for instance, that "there are mountains in the interior regions of India which are inaccessible to men, and therefore full of wild beasts; among them the Unicorn, which they call 'cartazan,' that has feet like those of the elephant and the tail of a goat. It is exceedingly swift of foot. Between its brows there stands a single horn. . . . It has great strength of body, and it is armed besides with an unconquerable horn. It seeks out the most deserted places and wanders there alone. They say that the young ones are sometimes taken to the king to be exhibited . . . but no one remembers the capture of a single specimen of mature age."[9]

Aelian attributed to the Unicorn some additional traits not mentioned by Ctesias or Aristotle. But it's obvious that he, too, although not doubting explicitly the existence of the Unicorn, was careful in choosing his words, and one wonders if he really believed the stories when he used the words "they say" or "no one remembers."

The same might be said about the passage in Julius Caesar's *The Gallic Wars*: "There is [in the Hercynian forest, in Germany] an ox, shaped like a stag, from the middle of whose forehead, between the ears, stands a single horn, taller and straighter than the horns we know."[10] Here again we have rumors that the author had heard about an unknown, uninhabited country or region, full of wonders and of strange creatures that apparently no one had ever seen and so no one could describe by analogy. Thus Pliny the Elder, in his *Historia Naturalium*, wrote about the Indians hunting "an exceedingly wild beast called the monocerous . . . that cannot be taken alive."[11] And thus many others, who borrowed their descriptions of the Unicorn from Aelian or Pliny, heard some rumors from travelers, added some traits of their own or from later books.

During the medieval period in Europe, the Unicorn appeared time and again in legends, in allegories, in bestiaries and psalters. He gained a new mode of existence that did not require any "scientific" proofs, any evidence by witnesses or direct observation. Yet, the wonder and doubts were not effaced; they merely reappeared in different disguises. In the late Renaissance, the Unicorn again became a subject of so-called scientific inquiry and research—and again a subject of doubts, speculations, riddles. A typical example of these books is *Historia Animalium* by the Swiss Conrad Gesner, which I've read in its translation into English by Edward Topsell (London 1607), entitled *Historie of Four-Footed Beasts*:

> We are now come to the history of a beast, whereof divers people in every age of the worlde have made great question, because of the rare vertues thereof; therefore it behooveth us to use some diligence in comparing together the several testimonies that are spoken of this beast, for the better satisfaction of such as are now alive, and clearing of the point for them that shall be born hereafter, whether there be a Unicorn; for that is the main question to be resolved.[12]

Later in this chapter on the Unicorn, Gesner (or Topsell) mentions the doubts that many people have about the existence of the Unicorn and supports his thesis that the Unicorn does exist with different sources, saying:

> . . . but of the true Unicorn, whereof there were more proofs in the world, because of the nobleness of his horn, they have ever been in doubt: by which distraction it appeareth unto me that *there is some secret enemy* in the inward degenerate nature of man, which continually blindeth the eyes of God his people, from beholding and believing the greatness of God his works. (*emphasis added*)[13]

Gesner and Topsell did know of the doubts that blind

the eyes of men from recognizing the truth about the existing Unicorn and describe his "virtues" as real, though rare. Yet the main proof is not based upon observation of nature, but upon the Bible:

> But to the purpose, that there is such a beast, the Scripture it self witnesseth, for *David* thus speaketh in the 92. Psalm: *Et erigetur cornu meum tanquam monocerotis.* That is, my horn shall be lifted up like the horn of a Unicorn; whereupon all Divines that ever wrote, have not only collected that there is a Unicorn, but also affirm the similitude to be betwixt the Kingdom of *David* and the horn of the Unicorn, that as the horn of the Unicorn is wholesome to all beasts and creatures, so should the Kingdom of *David* be in the generation of Christ; And do we think that *David* would compare the virtue of his Kingdome, and the powerful redemption of the world unto a thing that is not, or is uncertain and fantastical. . . .[14]

Actually, all the references in the Hebrew Bible, used by many Christian writers before Gesner and after him, are based on the word *Re'em*, or *Re'emim*, which appears in Numbers, Deuteronomy, Job, and the Psalms, and which was translated by the Septuagint (3rd century B.C.E.) as *monoceros*. The Vulgate translated the Greek *monokeros* with the word *Unicorn*.[2]* All Christian writers in other European languages used the Greek or Latin translations of the Old Testament as their source, not the Hebrew original. We don't know who or what the Re'em was, and how or why it was translated into *monokeros*. (As far as I know, there is no other translation of the word *Re'em*.) It is also not clear if the Re'em in the Hebrew

---

*Sometimes *monokeros* was translated in the Vulgate as *rhynoceros*.

Bible had one horn or two. In any case, the Re'em was a legendary animal who dwelt in a remote desert and was obviously a paradigm of a mighty yet unknown creature.

For Gesner, as for many other Christian interpreters and commentators on the Bible, the Re'em-as-Unicorn became the emissary of God or a symbol of his might. For them, the mere fact that the Re'em or, rather, his transformation into Monokeros or Unicorn, was irrefutable proof that the Unicorn really existed. Yet his existence remained a subject of doubts and arguments about his nature and other unresolved questions.

In his excellent book *The Lore of the Unicorn*, Odell Shepard dedicates a whole chapter to the "Battle of Books,"[15] where he discusses the battle among scholars in the 16th and 17th centuries over the existence of the Unicorn. The reasons for this battle, according to Shepard, may have been pragmatic, related to the use of the animal's horn as a means for healing, purifying, exonerating, or merely as precious treasure. Most of these scholars, some of whom were physicians, cited earlier writings about the Unicorn, and were mostly interested in the magic power of the horn. But even so, they were obliged first to prove that the Unicorn did exist. Some of them, on the other hand, living in an enlightened epoch, denied its existence, argued that it was a legend, a superstitious belief, basing their arguments on the wide discrepancies in the Unicorn tradition.

Such arguments could be applied, and were applied, to other mythical creatures, or to myth in general. The unique case of the Unicorn is demonstrated by the scholars who claimed to believe in his existence yet could not dispel their doubts. Moreover, whenever a scholar denied the veracity of the myth, he was opposed by other scholars who claimed that the Unicorn existed in nature, though they could not ignore the arguments against this belief.

Shepard quotes two writers, who published their books in the same year (1566), one denying the Unicorn's existence—Andrea Marini—and one claiming to believe in it—Andrea Bacci. The latter serves as an excellent example of the doubts that clung even to the most ardent believers. Bacci argued that the legend of the Unicorn differs from all other superstitions, since it had lasted longer. Superstitions, he wrote, live on the popular tongue alone, but the belief in the Unicorn has been maintained by the greatest writers, sacred and profane. He was not very accurate in this statement: most writers, both sacred and profane, did express their doubts, explicitly or implicitly, or evaded the question about the Unicorn's existence by planting him in a unique and peculiar kingdom, half imaginary or allegorical, half natural and "zoological." But even Bacci himself, who wanted to convince his readers that he was a firm believer in the reality of the Unicorn, found it necessary to add, according to Shepard, "The fact that the Unicorn is almost unknown does not argue its nonexistence but only its rarity. . . . Notices of the Unicorn continue to be confused merely because the beast is very wild and is not found in Europe."[16]

Farther on, Bacci wrote about the "due gran segreti della natura" and deciphered the first secret of nature by saying that there are very few creatures so distinguished in beauty, just "in order that God Almighty may have the greater glory in His works."[17] In a way, Bacci's argument recalls the answer of Jehovah to Job out of the whirlwind: "Will the Unicorn be willing to serve thee, or abide by thy crib? Canst thou bind the Unicorn with his band in the furrow? or will he harrow the valleys after thee? Wilt thou trust him, because his strength is great? How wilt thou leave thy labour to him? Wilt thou believe him, that he will bring home thy seed, and gather it into thy barn?" (Job 39: 9-12).

The Unicorn here is the Hebrew *Re'em*, and God mentioned him since he is both strong and mysterious, unknown to men. According to Bacci, "As Nature produces few individuals of the most wonderful kinds and the highest value . . . it follows that the

Unicorn, being so rare, must have a great value. . . . As a manifest proof of this, the animal has a strong instinct for solitude, living in deserts so remote that it seems almost a miracle whenever its horn is found."[18] However, Bacci compromises his reasons for defending a belief in the Unicorn by saying: "Whether the [Unicorn's horn] sweats or does not sweat, whether it makes water boil or does not make it boil, the belief that it does so will do no injury to truth and will be for the good of the state. . . . Thus the common good obliges us to write and to persuade the ignorant that what is said of the [Unicorn's horn] is true. . . ."[19]

According to Shepard, Bacci was probably motivated by the need to prove the exceptional merits of the horn, a very pragmatic need, and was probably concerned about his status as a physician to the pope, who used the horn as did many other dignitaries at that time. But I am more interested in his considerable and fascinating scholastic effort to prove the existence of the Unicorn by using a "scientific" language about the creature, thus adding to the controversies, doubts, and difficulties of coping with the question of whether or not the Unicorn really existed "in Nature." Bacci wrote, for example, that the Unicorn's horn "has much *forma* in proportion to its *materia*, and its matter, as in the case of gems, is so pure and splendid and starry that none can deny it a heavenly origin."[20] Despite their "scientific" quality, Bacci's words support the universal attitude toward the Unicorn as a heavenly, splendid and starry creature.

No matter, then, what Bacci's real motivations were in defending the notion of the Unicorn's "real" existence. The nature of his arguments coincides with the tradition of attitudes toward the Unicorn in all ages.

Shepard introduces other examples from the "Battle of the Books," of which I have chosen two. The first is Ambroise Paré's *Discours . . . de la licorne* (published in Paris in 1582):

In one place he wrote explicitly: "If so great varity of dissenting opinions easily induceth me to believe that this word Unicorne is not the proper name of any beast in the world, and that it is a thing only feigned by painters and writers." Somewhat later, however, in the *Discours*, he is obliged to consider the Biblical references to the animal, and these wrench from him the reluctant admission: *"Il faut donc croire qu'il des Licornes."*[21]

I believe that Paré speaks in the voice of a skeptic, one who found a refuge from his doubts in the Holy Scripture—if indeed he did.

We read a different way of arguing in behalf of the Unicorn in *Exercitations* (1557) by one of the most prominent scholars of the late Renaissance, Julius Caesar Scaliger. Shepard writes that

[Scaliger was] able to bear down almost any opinion by the sheer weight of his prestige. We have God's word, says he, to prove that the Unicorn existed at one time, and God cannot lie. If it existed once, then it exists still, for otherwise a vacuum would have been made in nature, which is absurd, for everyone knows that nature abhors a vacuum. Therefore unicorns exist.[22]

God's might and the Scriptures, nature's laws and the common good—all of these were recruited to prove the existence of the Unicorn, and all of them could not banish the doubts. Thus, Sir Thomas Browne, in his book of *Enquiries into Very Many Received Tenets and Commonly Presumed Truths*, Part III, Chapter 23 (published in London, 1646):

Wee are so farre from denying there is any Unicorne at all, that wee affirme there

are many kinds thereof. . . . Although we
concede there are many Unicornes, yet are
we still to seeke; for whereunto to affixe
this horne in question, or to determine
from which thereof we receive this magnified medecine, we have no assurance. . .
. [We cannot] be secure about what creature is meant thereby, what constant
shape it holdeth. . . . this animal is not uni-
formly described. . . .[23]

In the 18th and 19th centuries, the arguments
about the existence of the Unicorn in nature sub-
sided, though rumors about his appearance in exotic
countries—Africa, Tibet, even North America—still
continued. Yet a sober, rationalist writer like Samuel
Johnson translated a book called *A Voyage to
Abysinia*, by Father Jerome Lobo (London, 1735),
and wrote in his preface, "[What Father Lobo wrote]
whether true or not, is at least probable; and he who
tells nothing exceeding the bounds of probability has
a right to demand that they should believe him who
cannot contradict him. He [Father Lobo] appears to
have described things as he saw them, to have copied
Nature from the Life, and to have consulted his Senses, not his Imagination."[24] One may still ask
whether Johnson was honest in these words or ironic. The skepticism is certainly there, but also the
wish to believe.

Another rationalist, the philosopher Leibniz, in
his *Protogaea* (1749) admitted that he doubted the
real existence of the Unicorn; but a supposed skele-
ton of the Unicorn, found in a quarry near Quedlin-
berg, Germany, in 1663, and another, seen by Leibniz, which was found in 1740 in the Einhornloch at
Scharzfeld in the Harz Mountains, converted him
and convinced him that the Unicorn had really existed, although it did not exist anymore.[25]

Doubts and denials about the Unicorn have followed him since the early beginning of his myth.
What distinguishes them from the attitude toward

other myths is this strange mixture of incredulity and the manifested, consistent will—quite often, of the same skeptics and heretics—to believe in the existence of the Unicorn in spite of all doubts and rational observation of nature. We read for instance about Apollonius of Tyana, a Roman philosopher from the School of Pythagoras in the 1st century B.C.E., who traveled in many countries, including India and was attracted to Oriental magic and legends. According to his biographer, Philostratus, he had seen the one-horned Indian asses and was told about the magic power of their horns. But when Damis, one of the philosopher's companions, asked him what he thought about these stories, he answered: "I should have believed it if I had found that the kings of this country were immortal."[26]

Shakespeare mentioned the Unicorn in three of his plays, and in the poem *The Rape of Lucrece*. Did he believe in the Unicorn's existence? In one play, *Timon of Athens*, it seems that Shakespeare followed the common tradition: "Wert that the Unicorn, pride and wrath would confound thee and make thine own self the conquest of thy fury" (IV: 3). In *Julius Caesar*, Decius Brutus says about Caesar, "He loves to hear that Unicorns may be betrayed with trees" (II: 1). It is hard to decide whether these mocking words assert or doubt the real existence of the Unicorn. Yet in *The Tempest* Sebastian says, "Now I will believe that there are Unicorns" (III: 3). The wise and omniscient Shakespeare here strikes at the core of the Unicorn's existence: now I'll believe, since there is a place, a world created by the imagination (or Prospero's magic) where Unicorns can exist.

If the Unicorn disappeared from nature, and cannot be mapped in zoological charts, it certainly has not vanished from the domain of imagination. I have found him, for instance, in Ariosto's *Orlando Furioso*, "as white as lilies or unmelten snow, deckt with so great pride."[27] In Keats's *Endymion*, and later in a sonnet of Mallarmé:

But near the window void Northwards, a
gold dies down composing perhaps a
decor of Unicorns kicking sparks at a nixie.
She, nude and defunct in the mirror, while yet,
in the oblivion caused by the frame there
     appears
of scintillations at once the septent.[28]

And Rilke, before writing about the creature that
never was, saw him this way:

The ivory undercarriage of the legs
maintained an easy balance as it moved,
a white brilliance slid blissfully through the
     coat,
and on the brow, on the quiet, lucid brow,
the bright horn stood, like a moonlit tower,
and every footstep carried it erect.
. . . .
But its gaze, intercepted by no object,
cast images far into space
and brought a blue legend-cycle to a close.[29]

Here, then, was the kingdom of the Unicorns.

Do they still exist in the 20th century? In Tennessee Williams's play *The Glass Menagerie*, Laura
tells Jim that "the Unicorn is my favorite," and Jim
answers, "Unicorns?—Aren't they extinct in the
modern world?"[30]

Apparently not. The Unicorn does exist in Laura's
glass menagerie, but he's broken. He appears in Jean
Cocteau's ballet *Lady with the Unicorn*, but when the
lady's mirror shows him the visage of the knight who
brings her love, the Unicorn dies.

We read in W.H. Auden's *New Year Letter:*

O Unicorn among the cedars,
To whom no magic charm can lead us.
White childhood moving like a sigh
Through the green woods unharmed in thy
Sophisticated innocence,
To call thy true love to the dance.[31]

And in another poem, *Shibboleth*, by Paul Celan, we read:

> *Einhorn:*
> *du weist un die steine*
> *du weist un die wasser*
> *komm,*
> *ich führ dich hinweg*
> *zu den stimmen*
> *von Estremadura.*

> (Unicorn:
> you know about the stones
> you know about the water
> come,
> for you I'll go
> to the voices
> from Estremadura.)[32]

Auden did see his Unicorn "move like a sigh through the green woods," though "no magic charm" could lead him to it. Celan calls the Unicorn to lead him to the voices from Estremadura, whether a real or imaginary place. For both of them, as for many other poets and artists, antique and modern, the Unicorn has existed somehow, somewhere, yet not physically, or it has remained a longing, a dream, a call from another world.

In my search for the Unicorn, I have not been concerned with the question of whether he exists, or existed, in nature. My main interest is the question: What endowed the Unicorn with a unique character that distinguished him from other myths and has induced so many poets and artists, across different epochs and cultures, to bestow on him the power to exist-and-not-exist, to appear and disappear and reappear, to live and die and resurrect, as no other natural or mythical creature has ever done?

After three years of searching for the Unicorn, I cannot pretend that I've found him, or the answers to my questions. Very often I have followed my guides to a museum, a church, and discovered that he had disappeared, was erased from a wall on which I'd been told I'd find him, stolen from a place where he should have been; had been rooted out from a tombstone leaving behind only the socket wherein he'd rested before. When I searched for him in books, ancient and medieval, or in illustrations of old manuscripts, I've often discovered that he was depicted there in many variations, contradicting each other or differing totally from the images they were meant or promised to expose.

At the end of my voyage, I was left with questions, riddles, wonders. Yet the Unicorn himself is always there—in legends and poems, paintings and tapestries—and always representing the paradox of a creature that never was—yet firmly and clearly exists, no less real than nature itself.

Notes

1. Rainer Maria Rilke, *Sämtliche Werke* I, *Die Sonette an Orpheus* (Frankfurt: Insel, 1955) 2: 4. My translation was helped by the translation of A. Poulin, Jr.: Rainer Maria Rilke, *Duino Elegies and the Sonnets to Orpheus* (Boston: Houghton Mifflin, 1977) 145.

2. See Odell Shepard, *The Lore of the Unicorn* (New York: Harper, 1979) 286, *n*30. A detailed description of the Chinese Unicorn and his various names and characters is included in Charles Gould's *The Unicorn: Mythical Monsters* (London: Allen, 1886) 348-365.

3. Jorge Luis Borges, *The Book of Imaginary Beings*, rev. and trans. Norman Thomas de Giovanni in collaboration with the author (New York: Dutton, 1969) 228-229.

4. Quoted from Margoulies's *Anthologie raisonée de la littératur chinoise* (1948) in Borges, *Book of Imaginary Beings*, 232-233.

5. N. McLeod, *Epitome of the Ancient History of Japan*; quoted in Shepard, 96.

6. Ctesias, *La Perse, L'Inde*, trans. R.H. Henry (Brussels: Office de Publicité, 1947) 80. Ctesias wrote his book in 398 B.C.E. A fragmentary abstract of it was made by Photius, Patriach of Constantinople, in the 9th century C.E. Ctesias had probably seen the Ishtar Gate in Babylon

(now in the Bode Museum, Berlin), where one-horned beasts are advancing toward the gate.

7. Ctesias, *La Perse*, 82.

8. Aristotle, *De Historia Animalium* II, 2.8, trans. A.L. Peck (Cambridge, MA: Harvard UP, 1973) 221.

9. Aelian, *De Historia Animalium*, III, 44; IV, 52; XVI, 20; quoted in Alwyn Scholfield, *On the Characteristics of Animals* (Cambridge, MA: Harvard UP, 1959) 3: 289*ff.*

10. Julius Ceasar, *De Bello Gallico* VI, 26, trans. H.J. Edward, *The Gallic War* (London: Heinemann, 1917) 351-352.

11. Pliny the Elder, *Historia Naturalium* VIII, 3, trans. H.J. Rackman, *Natural History*, (Cambridge, MA: Harvard UP, 1956) 857.

12. Edward Topsell, *Historie of Foure-Footed Beasts*, (New York, Da Capo, 1967) 551. I have modernized the spelling.

13. Topsell, *Historie*, 552.

14. Topsell, 552.

15. Shepard, *Lore*, 155-190.

16. Shepard, 164.

17. Shepard, 164.

18. Shepard, 165.

19. Shepard, 167.

20. Shepard, 167.

21. Shepard, 184.

22. Shepard, 194.

23. Shepard, 179.

24. Shepard, 199-200.

25. Shepard, 190.

26. Shepard, 39.

27. Ludivico Ariosto, *Orlando Furioso*, Book 6, Canto 69, trans. Sir John Harington (New York: Oxford UP, 1972) 66.

28. Stéphane Mallarmé, *Poems*, trans. Roger Fry (New York: New Directions, 1951) 104-107.

29. R.M. Rilke, *The Unicorn: New Poems, 1907*, trans. Edward Snow (San Francisco: North Point, 1984) 77.

30. Tennessee Williams, *The Glass Menagerie* (New York: Signet, 1987) 121.

31. W.H. Auden, *The Collected Poetry* (New York: Random House, 1945) 315.

32. Paul Celan, *Shibboleth* (Frankfurt: Suhrkamp, 1969) 48.

The Most Human of Them All

Aussi comme unicorne sui
Qui s'esbahist en regardant
Quant la pucele va mirant
Tant est liee son ennui,
Pasmee chiet en son giron;
Lors l'ocit on en traison.
Et moi ont mort d'utel semblant
Amors et ma dame, por voir:
Mon coeur ont, n'en puis point ravoir

Thibaut de Champagne, roi de Navarre[1]

"I too am like the Unicorn / who pauses in amaze / when he the maiden sees." These lines, written by Thibaut IV de Champagne in the first half of the 13th century, could indeed serve as a motto for my book about the Unicorn. They expose the central theme or concept in the vast verbal and visual literature about the Unicorn in the era of his myth's greatest flourishing: between the 10th and the 16th centuries, but also long before and after. The images, the accentuations, usually differed from one period to another, from one culture to another. To grasp the full meaning of the poems and paintings from this period, we should know the specific and thematic traditions. We should probably try to survey and understand the interaction between several concepts of love, religious and artistic attitudes toward the legendary "bestiary" and the relation of these beasts to men in late medieval times and in the Renaissance.

But beneath all the various representations and interpretations we may conclude without doubt that the Unicorn was the most human of all mythical creatures. Its "human" character could be expressed by different means: direct analogy between him and man, metaphorical affinity, hints of physical resemblance, allusions to similar destiny. In several cases we even find advice or instruction to human beings to regard the Unicorn as a paradigm for their behavior and destiny. Thus we read in the following lines, written in the 13th century:

Daz aingehurn dy natur hat,
Aller raynikagt is nach gat.
Also sol der mensch sein perayt
Mit aller rechten raynikagt.

(The Unicorn has such a nature,
that he has got all purity in him.
So man also should carry on
with all the right purity.)[2]

In most of his representations, the Unicorn appears as a paradigm of humanity's quest for beauty, strength, nobility, pride. Yet, on the other hand, he represents other aspects of human character and fate: he is a vulnerable creature, often betrayed by love or innocence, often punished for his desires and deviations. Human he remains, in all cases.

In my search for the Unicorn, I wondered how and why he acquired those human merits and faults, more than any other mythical creature I know about. I found one answer, as could be expected, in ancient Indian legends about the Unicorn (the first stories that exist in writing). Thus in Book 3 of the *Mahabharata: The Book of the Forest*,[3] we read about Rsyasrnga ("antelope horn"), a boy who bore the horn of an antelope on his brow, and about his fate and adventures—a story that already includes many elements of the much later legends about the Unicorn.

Rsyasrnga, a mythical creature, was born to the Brahmin seer Vibhandaka, a hermit who "had perfected his soul with austerities."[4] One day, the tale goes, when the seer had gone to a lake and was engaged in his austerities, he saw the apsara Vrvasi, and his seed spilled forth on the lake water. (According to other, earlier versions, Vibhandaka, or Kasyvapa, as he was sometimes called, spilled his seed on the water when he saw a stag copulating with a doe.) A thirsty doe swallowed the seed along with the water and gave birth to the son of Vibhandaka, who was called Rsyasrnga because he had one horn on his brow.

The great-spirited child grew up in the same isolated forest as his father. Other than his father, he had never seen a human being, and his mind was set on a life of chastity, but as the story continues, we learn that Rsyasrnga was destined (condemned? blessed?) to escape from his isolated dwelling. When Lomapada, the King of Anga, banished the Brahamins from his land, "the Thousand-Eyed God" stopped the rains, and the sole means to bring the rains back was to fetch the hermit's son Rsyasrnga—a forest child, ignorant of women and devoted to uprightness—and bring him to Anga.

The only device for fetching him was to send into the forest a beautiful and witty courtesan to seduce Rsyasrnga. And so she did—first with words, then with "fragrant garlands . . . colorful and flamboyant clothes, and the finest liquors; and then she laughed and happily played about . . . and seductively touching his limbs with hers; embraced Rsyasrnga . . .and shamelessly . . . she continued seducing the seer's son."[5] But when she saw that Rsyasrnga desired her, she retreated and left him alone, crazy with love, "heaving many sighs, disturbed and given to brooding—the picture of grief."[6]

According to the story in the Mahabharata, Rsyasrnga did not know that the temptress was a girl. When his father asked him who had come to visit him, he answered that "a student came . . . full of spirit . . . as radiant as a son of the gods."[7] Since he'd never seen any human being except his father until then, he thought that he would continue to practice awesome austerity together with his new friend, to whom he was attracted by "his" marvelous appearance and words, by "the beautiful fragrance of his body," and by his heavenly spirit.[8]

The story-poem in the Mahabharata might be read, then, as a story of first love, or awakening desire of a young hermit. As befits such a story, the wise father knows, of course, who the visitor was, and tells his son: "They [women in general, or courtesans] are demons, who stalk the earth in all their wondrously beautiful shapes. They are peerlessly lovely and very cruel, and plot to prevent austerities. . . . A self-controlled hermit must not frequent them at all."[9]

But, as happens in good stories about youthful love, Rsyasrnga did not listen to his father's warning, went hunting for the courtesan, sought her for three days, and when he failed to find her, returned to his hermitage; but when the father went to the forest, in his ascetic fashion, the courtesan returned to the hermitage and succeeded in seducing the young hermit and bringing him with her to the king's palace.

The moment he arrived, the god began to rain forth, and the earth was filled with water. When the king, Lomapada, saw that his wishes were fulfilled, he gave his daughter Santa to Rsyasrnga.

This story about Rsyasrnga can be approached as a rich love story with a happy ending. But it also includes several elements that relate him, on the one hand, to other Indian mythical legends—to which I'll return later—and, on the other hand, to the unique myth of the Unicorn. Rsyasrnga is endowed with a mythical horn, destined to bring rain and fertility to the earth. He was born to a divine doe in a supernatural way. Thus he really belongs to two different spheres, the human and the mythical, and wanders always between them, representing both.

In his way, Rsyasrnga is an example of human nature, yielding to temptations, cheated and betrayed. At the same time he might be perceived as the projection of human aspiration to be superhuman: to be endowed with superhuman qualities like the magical horn and with other elements that hint at his divine character.

The Indian mythical stories about the human-Unicorn, after the Jaminiya-Upanishad-Brahamaya, from 800 B.C.E. on, and throughout all of their variations and deviations, imply the contradictory nature of this mythical creature: he lives in solitude, but is seduced into searching out the company of other creatures; he is ascetic but tempted by eros; he has one horn, a symbol of power and virility, but having a horn may also be a punishment for the father's outburst of sexual desire or a sign of weakness; his asceticism is the cause of draught but he is the one who causes the rain to fall; he is tempted by a courtesan but believes that he was enticed by a male hermit and thus maintains his holiness; he follows a courtesan but marries the king's daughter; he returns to his ascetic solitude but his loving wife follows him there.

The story in the Mahabharata is one version of similar and more ancient Indian stories about the human-Unicorn. It could be read as a part of Indian mythology and understood as such. Its similarity to stories about Siva underline this connection. But it also provides us with certain clues to the ways later myths about the Unicorn evolved. There are many similarities between the Indian stories and later European and Arabian ones about the Unicorn. In all of them, he is "the most human" of all mythical creatures. In all of them, the Unicorn represents the ambiguities and contradictions that signify man's attitude toward a myth he himself created. We may say, of course, that this is true about any other mythical creature. All of them may be perceived as projections of human nature, yet separated from the human by their supernatural qualities. But the moment they appear as mythical, they remain in their separate and non-human sphere. The Unicorn is probably the only mythical creature that exists in the domain between myth and human life. (Throughout my essay I ignore the vampire, a mythical/human figure, true, but one of a lesser order.)

In all of the Indian stories, the human-Unicorn is hidden, unknown to men, and unwilling or forbidden to reveal himself. And in all of them, he acquires his human nature when he comes out of his seclusion, reveals himself, and participates in human life. Yet, when he is revealed and behaves like an ordinary human being, he loses his mythical-mystical character, and therefore must return to his hidden place and mysterious mode of existence in order to stay alive.

In the Mahabharata story, as in earlier Indian versions, the father warns his son against the wiles of women, who will seduce him into being human and destroy his chastity and ascetic seclusion. But the women in some of these stories are the asparas, sent by Indra himself. It is not clear whether the asparas are only good and pure or also evil. It seems, then, as if Rsyasrnga (or Isisinga, in the Jataka) needed the love of the aspara in order to learn who he was. Therefore he forgave the aspara who seduced him, blessed her, and returned to his hermitage.[10]

In one Jataka,[11] the god Indra was afraid of the powers of the human-Unicorn Isisinga and his *tapas* (austerities); therefore, he stopped the rains for three years and told the king: "Send your daughter Nalinka to break the virtue of Isisinga and it will rain."[12] Nalinka enticed Isisinga, his virtue was overcome, his meditation broken off, and he made love to her. Then she ran away from him, and Indra sent rain that day. Isisinga longed for Nalinka, still thinking that she too was an ascetic hermit, until his father realized that a woman had broken his son's virtue and warned Isisinga to beware of the "female demon," and Isisinga returned to his seclusion and meditation.

All these stories, of course, could be told about a young human hermit who is awakened by eros, tempted by a woman, and has magical powers to stop the rain or bring it forth. (In some, merely the appearance of the devoted hermit among men brought the rain. In others, only when the sexual union between the hermit and the woman took place did the rains come.) But Rsyasrnga and Isisinga also belong to the mythical sphere, and participate in a broader and more universal drama, where gods and their emissaries play roles. The horn of Rsyasrnga or Isisinga has, then, a double character: it is a symbol both of the phallus, of sexual desire, and simultaneously of relations with divine powers, their demands and rules.

In most of the Indian texts, and in the Jatakas, the ascetic nature of the hermit Unicorn prevails, and he abandons the woman and returns to his *tapas*. According to the Ramayana and the Padma Purana, he remains with Santa, or Nalini, the king's daughter, and does not return to the forest. The story in the Mahabharata suggests a compromise of considerable significance: Rsyasrnga does return to the forest, but his wife follows him there. Thus the ambiguous character of the human-Unicorn, half-human and half-mythical, is maintained.

The Indian stories about the Unicorn deal directly with a human creature endowed with the appearance of a Unicorn. But some of the components of these stories are present in later myths of the Unicorn, where he appears as an animal with one horn, yet behaves in ways similar to those of the Indian human-Unicorn. Like him, the animal-Unicorn is secluded, then tempted by a woman, and then is either taken to the king's palace or returns to his seclusion.

Heinrich Luders, in his article "Die Sage von Rsyasrnga" (1897), argued that this story is the non-Christian source of many Christian legends about the Unicorn.[13] In his *Romantic Legend of Sakya Buddhism*, Samuel Beal wrote: "The connection of this myth with the medieval story of the Unicorn being capable of capture only by a chaste woman is too evident to require proof."[14] Many other scholars accepted this opinion, even though it still needs proof. (According to Ctesias, the face of the Unicorn resembles the human face: his ears and eyes look like human ears and eyes. Did Ctesias know the Indian story of the human-Unicorn?)

I admit I've not found proof of the assumption that the Indian stories were the direct source of the later European ones about the Unicorn. And if they were, I don't know how they were transferred and transformed into the later myths. It is quite possible that the Indian myth, or some of its ingredients, wandered from India to Persia and from there to the Hellenistic world, and was revived in Medieval and Renaissance art and poetry.

It is also possible that the European-Christian myths of the Unicorn were begotten and developed independently of the Indian ones, yet were nourished and inspired by needs, impulses, and aspirations similar to those that gave birth to the Indian myths, and through their growth, probably assimilated some components of the ancient Indian myths and transferred them to new ones. In my search for the Unicorn, for instance, I found in Midrash Tanhuma (fourth or fifth century C.E.) a story about Cain, saying that the mark mentioned in Genesis 4:15 was really a horn on his brow, intended to save his life. But according to the Midrash, the horn did not save Cain, and he was killed by his great-grandson Lamech, who was probably frightened when he saw this exceptional creature with one horn.

There is no way to tell where and how this story was begotten, whether it was influenced by some wandering legends about the human-Unicorn or arose independently. In any case, there are many similarities between the Indian myths and the European ones, the most striking of which is the human nature of the Unicorn, although in the European myth he is an animal, not human shaped. Thus we read in the Syrian version of the *Physiologus*, the most popular and most important source of all medieval legends about the Unicorn:

> There is an animal called dajja, extremely gentle, which the hunters are unable to capture because of its great strength. It has in the middle of its brow a single horn. But observe the ruse by which the huntsmen take it. They lead forth a young virgin, pure and chaste, to whom, when the animal sees her, he approaches, throwing himself upon her. Then the girl offers him her breasts, and the animal begins to suck the breasts of the maiden and

to conduct himself familiarly with her. Then the girl, while sitting quietly, reaches forth her hand and grasps the horn on the animal's brow, and at this point the huntsmen come up and take the beast and go away with him to the king.[15]

J.W. Einhorn, in his book *Spiritalis Unicornis*, mentions scores of scholars who wrote about the *Physiologus* and argued about its authentic version—if there was one—and the dates of its composition and its sources. Likewise, he mentions the hundreds of versions of the *Physiologus*, as well as hundreds of illustrations of the story quoted above, and the variety of later interpretations. In all these versions, interpretations, and illustrations, the central components remain the same: an imaginary animal, one-horned, secluded and unseen, is attracted to a maiden, tempted and captured by her, and brought to the king's palace.

From the Indian stories we know much more about the life and behavior of the human-Unicorn *before* he was tempted by a woman, as well as the reason he was brought to the king's palace. Those two elements of the *Physiologus* story were developed and gained their symbolical meanings later on. The central element, the capture by a woman, is certainly the clearest and strongest allusion to the human character of the Unicorn, both in the Indian stories and the *Physiologus*. And this was the theme that attracted so many poets and artists to the Unicorn and to the analogy between him and the human.

I've picked at random only a few examples from the vast medieval literature that derived from the story in the *Physiologus* and played with the theme that accentuates the human aspect of the Unicorn. Thus, for example, a poem, "The Unicorn," by Phillipe de Thaon (1121-1135):

> *Monoceros, beast that's born*
> *With on its head one horn . . .*

By a virgin it is caught;
If men would hunt it as prey
And catch and take it away,
Into the forest they hie
Where its deep haunt doth lie;
And there a virgin is placed,
Her breasts outside her waist;
And by the fragrance about,
Monoceros smells her out.
He then to the virgin wends
Kisses her breasts and bends
To fall asleep on them,
Thus cometh his death to him.[16]

And again, in *Le Bestiaire Divin*, by Guillaume, clerc de Normandie (13th century)—one of the most popular bestiaries in medieval times—we read:

> The Unicorn has but one horn in the middle of its forehead. Hunters can catch the Unicorn only by placing a young virgin in its haunts. No sooner does he see the damsel, than he runs toward her, and lies down at her feet and suffers himself to be captured by the hunters.[17]

In *Le Bestiaire d'Amour* by Richard de Fournival (c. 1260), the analogy between the man and the Unicorn is more explicit:

> I have been drawn to you by your sweet odour alone, as the Unicorn falls asleep under the influence of a maiden's fragrance.* For this is the nature of the Unicorn, that no other beast is so hard to capture . . . so that no one dares to go forth against him except a virgin girl. And as soon as he is made aware of her presence

---

*The fragrance is mentioned also in the *Mahabharata*, as one of the devices to seduce the hermit-boy.

by the scent of her, he kneels humbly before her and humiliates himself as though to signify that he would serve her.

Therefore wise huntsmen who know his nature set a virgin in his way; he falls asleep in her lap; and while he sleeps the hunters come up and kill him.

Even so has love dealt cruelly with me; for I have been the proudest man alive with regard to love, and I have thought never to see the woman I should care to possess. . . . But love, the skilled huntsman, has set in my path a maiden in the odour of whose sweetness I have fallen asleep, and I die the death to which I was doomed.[18]

In one of the best-known epics of the Middle Ages, *Parzifal*, by Wolfram von Eschenbach, we read:

*ein Tier heizt Monicirus
daz erkennt der megede Reine so groz
daz her slaefet uf der megede Schoz.*

[A beast there is, Monoceros,
Which deems young maids so innocent
That on their laps 'twill sleep content.][19]

As the story goes on, however, we learn that the Unicorn does not "sleep content" in the maiden's lap. The lady in this epic says, "My greatly desired one was like the Unicorn in faithfulness, he is the animal whom the maidens should lament, for he was slain through purity." The last words of the lady are "I was his heart, he was my life".[20]

Thibault de Champagne, Richard de Fournival, and Wolfram von Eschenbach of course wrote about chivalric love, its nobility and sorrow, purity and death. They found the story of the Unicorn to be the most appropriate symbol of this kind of love, and thus adorned the human love with mythical traits;

or, if we wish, made the Unicorn story closer to human aspects of love.

In the Indian stories, the temptress maiden is sometimes a courtesan, sometimes the king's daughter. Likewise, in the later European stories about the maiden who captures the Unicorn, she may appear in different disguises: sometimes a noble virgin, chaste and pure, sometimes a prostitute, willingly collaborating with the hunters who capture and kill the Unicorn.

In the story *La Dame à la Lycorne et du Biau Chevalier au Lyon* (end of the 13th century), we read about the daughter of the king of Friesland who was so beauteous and charming, so superlatively good, pure, and chaste that the god of love bestowed on her a Unicorn. She remained faithful to the Unicorn till the end of the story.[21]

In a poem from *Des Knaben Wunderhorn*, an adaptation of medieval lore by Achim von Arnim, we read:

> *With sunbeams shining my pursuers,*
> *Like unicorn free do I bound,*
> *'Til even away from my torturers,*
>
> *To virgin's lap escape I've found,*
> *To match me with gossamer she knew*
> *But with the dawn she set me free.*[22]

But Johannes a San Geminiamo (1364) used the example of the Unicorn against the temptations of the whore. For this purpose he quoted the words of Proverbs (5:3-8):

> For the lips of a strange woman drop as an honeycomb, and her mouth is smoother than oil; But her end is bitter as wormwood, sharp as a two-edged sword. Her feet go down to death, her steps take hold on hell. . . . [Therefore] Remove thy way far from her, and come not nigh the door of her house.

He compared the whore of Proverbs to the evil woman who helps catching the Unicorn.[23]

Quite often, it's not at all clear if the maiden's role is traitorous or loving, as we read in the *Bestiaires* of Pierre de Beauvais:

> La mescine li oevre son giron. Et la beste flicist ses jambs devant la mescine, et met son cief en son giron tout simplement; et si s'endort ens.

> [The maiden opens her bosom. And the beast rests his feet in front of the maiden, and puts his head in her bosom quite simply; and there he falls asleep].[24]

The same ambiguity about the maiden's role appears also in some Arabian stories, whether influenced by the *Physiologus* or derived from other sources. Al-Tawhidi wrote about the Harish (one of the Arabian names for the Unicorn), that "it is necessary to use a strategem for seizing it, namely, to expose to its view a young virgin or a young girl. When it sees her, it jumps into her arms as though intending to suck her milk, which is a natural mark of affection ingrained in its nature. It sucks her breast, though there is no milk in them, with such a gusto that it is overpowered by intoxication, like the intoxication from wine. While it is in that state, the hunter comes and ties it up firmly with a rope. . . ."[25]

But according to the *Manafi* (1297?), the Harish is sucking the breasts of a beautiful girl who has been sent from a brothel to tempt him with her breasts. The Harish sucks the breasts "for about an hour and then falls asleep from the milk." It seems that the author himself was bewildered by the story and could not make up his mind about the maiden. Therefore he ends it with the exclamation, "Allah knows best."[26]

The human character of the Unicorn, especially through his relationship with a woman, was represented not only in stories and poems, but also in paintings, frescoes, tapestries and engravings during the Middle Ages. Many of them were direct or indirect illustrations of the *Physiologus* or the bestiaries influenced by it. In most of them, the behavior of both Unicorn and maiden is ambiguous, or has a double character.

In an early illustration of the *Physiologus* from the 10th century, there are two parts. In the first, the maiden is sitting and the Unicorn is resting his head in her lap. In the second, she is leading him to the king's palace, but we cannot tell for what purpose: to become his wife? to let him be killed? to keep him there as a captive? In a French coffret from the 14th century, the maiden is sweet-looking, innocent, smiling happily, but while she is holding the Unicorn's head in her lap, the hunters arrive and kill him, obviously with her willing collaboration.

In a Pisanello etching (now in the Uffizi in Florence), the hunters are chasing the Unicorn with hounds, and the maiden holds up her hand as if saying "Keep away," and covers the Unicorn with her coat to protect him. Yet she is the cause of his being captured. In the fresco of Falconetto (in St. Pietro Martire, Verona), the hunters are an angel at one side of the fresco and a Roman soldier at the other. Giorgione called his painting of the Unicorn *Allegory of Chastity* (now in the Rijksmuseum, Amsterdam), and it's not clear who is the chaste one, the maiden or the Unicorn. In Moretto's painting *The Holy Justina* (now in the Kunsthistorisches Museum, Vienna), she may be holy, but the scene is certainly erotic.

In some works, the Unicorn is chased by hunters. In others, he is captured by the woman. She may appear as a mother, a noble lady, a virgin, a saint, a prostitute. Sometimes she is the "wild lady," riding on the back of the Unicorn, and this might represent a faithful devotion or a mischievous wish to submit the Unicorn to her whims. We cannot tell why the Unicorn approaches the woman: yielding to erotic de-

Pisanello, *The Unicorn, the Hunters, and a Maiden*
(etching, Palazo Uffizi, Florence)

sire? seeking shelter?

Obviously we may attribute the affinity or analogy between the Unicorn and the human to the phallic symbolism of the horn. This was done in a humorous-satirical way by Rabelais in *Gargantua and Pantagruel*:

> I saw thirty-two unicorns [in The Land of Satin]. These were extraordinary vicious beasts, in every respect like thoroughbred horses—and, out of their foreheads, grew a sharp black horn, usually dangled down like a turkey-cock's crest, but when the unicorn meant to fight or to use it for any other purpose, it thrust it out, straight and hard as an arrow.
>
> Panurge assured me that he, too, possessed a horn, growing out, not from the middle of his forehead but somewhat lower down. It was comparable to the unicorn's, if not in length, at least in its virtues and properties. "When you're married, we'll try this out on your wife," cried Friar John.[27]

A simplistic attitude toward the erotic "symbolism" of the Unicorn can be seen in Gustave Moreau's paintings of *La Dame à la Unicorne*. Moreau was surely inspired by the famous tapestries in the Musée Cluny, bearing the same title. But in these tapestries, the relationship between the lady and Unicorn is ambiguous and the erotic aspect alluded to subtly. Even in the panel where the lady holds the Unicorn's horn in her hand, her face is turned away from the Unicorn, as if she hesitates to yield to her erotic desire, or as if she is afraid of the lion who stands there watching her. In Moreau's paintings, eros wins without restraint. In one of them, the lady is half naked, wearing an open robe and a hat. One of her hands is on the Unicorn's neck, and the other is holding a bouquet of flowers she has put on his neck.

Falconetto, *Annunciation* (fresco, Church of St. Pietro Martire, Verona)

Gustave Moreau, *La Dame à la Unicorne* (painting, Musée Gustave Moreau, Paris)

In another painting, though, the lady is still decently dressed, her two arms placed on the necks of two Unicorns. But another woman there is lying almost totally naked, and the Unicorn, embraced by her hand, is looking at her erotically, ready to launch the act of love.

Aubrey Beardsley, in the eighth chapter of *The Story of Venus and Tannhäuser, or "Under the Hill,"* which he called a "romantic novel," is more direct, perhaps pornographic, in describing the relation between the lady, in this case Queen Venus, and the Unicorn:

> When all was said and done, the Chevalier [Tannhäuser] tripped off to bid good morning to Venus. . . . He kissed her lightly upon the neck.
>
> "I'm just going to feed Adolphe," she said, pointing to a little reticule of buns that hung from her arm. Adolphe was her pet Unicorn. "He is such a dear," she continued; "milk-white all over excepting his black eyes, rose mouth and nostrils, and scarlet John."
>
> The Unicorn had a very pretty palace of its own, made of green foliage and golden bars—a fitting home for such a delicate and dainty beast. Ah, it was indeed a splendid thing to watch the white creature roaming in its artful cage, proud and beautiful, and knowing no mate except the Queen herself.
>
> "You mustn't come in with me—Adolphe is so jealous," she said . . . "but you can stand outside and look on; Adolphe likes an audience." . . . When the last crumbs had been scattered, Venus brushed her hands together and pretended to leave the cage. . . . Every morning she went through this piece of play, and every morning the amorous Unicorn was cheat-

Giorgione, *Allegory of Chastity* (painting, Rijksmuseum, Amsterdam)

ed into a distressing agony lest that day should have proved the last day of Venus's love. Not for long, though, would she leave him in that doubtful, piteous state, but running back passionately to where he stood, made adorable amends for her unkindness.

Poor Adolphe! How happy he was, touching the Queen's breasts with his quick   tongue-tip.
. . . Anyhow, Adolphe sniffed as never a man did around the skirts of Venus. After the first charming interchange of affectionate delicacies was over, the Unicorn lay down upon his side and, closing his eyes, beat his stomach wildly with the mark of manhood.

Venus caught that stunning member in her hands and lay her cheek along it; but few touches were wanted to consummate the creature's pleasure.[28]

These examples—and many other stories, poems, drawings, and paintings across the ages—may lead us, then, to the conclusion that the human character of the Unicorn derives from, or refers to, the erotic aspect of this creature, symbolized by its phallic horn. It is doubtlessly an inciting speculation, and easily applied to many of the Unicorn's representations in art and poetry.

Yet it is too simple-minded a theory, too narrow, and does not answer many questions about the impulse that drove the imagination of artists and poets to perceive the Unicorn as analogous to the human, nor does it cover many of the representations of the Unicorn, its nature, behavior, destiny. The myth of the Unicorn, as well as its analogy to man, is much wider, much more complicated and ambiguous than a simplistic phallic symbolism can cover and explain. It was already much broader and more complex in the ancient Indian myth and the chivalric poems of

Moretto, *The Holy Justina* (painting, Kunsthistorisches Museum, Vienna)

the late Middle Ages. It certainly remains complex and enigmatic in some modern manifestations of the analogy between the Unicorn and the human.

The urge to find an analogy between the Unicorn and the human in modern times can be found in many works of art and literature. But in most of them, the analogy is not merely based on the erotic aspect. In 1933, a Swedish zoologist named Bengt Berg, who also photographed a buck in profile so as to produce a picture of a Unicorn, quoted a refrain that he claimed to have found among the hymns of Buddha:

> *Like a lion, without fear of the howling pack,*
> *Like a gust of wind, ne'er trapped in a snare,*
> *Like a lotus blossom, ne'er sprinkled by water,*
> *Like me, like a Unicorn, in solitude roam.*[29]

Obviously the zoologist-poet was attracted not by the erotic aspect of the Unicorn, but by his habit or inclination to live in solitude, to hide, as we find in many other representations of this creature. In 1963 Iris Murdoch published her novel *The Unicorn*, about a lonely woman in a remote castle whose obsessional seclusion and fate implicitly allude to the story of the Unicorn. The erotic element is hinted at in this novel too, but it is not the main allusion of the analogy.

An Austrian painter, Ernst Fuchs, explained his paintings of the Unicorn in Freudian terms:

> The unicorn is *my* animal. I was the unicorn within me. The unicorn was *id*, the spirit that was driving me on. I painted it in the greatest variety of phases of its metamorphosis and continued to portray its passion, which I was indeed experiencing in my own life. . . .[30]

Ernest Fuchs was also concerned with the "variety of phases" of the Unicorn's metamorphoses" that

Leonardo da Vinci, *The Maiden and the Unicorn*
(etching, Ashmolean Museum, Oxford)

mark the unique character of this creature. As well as the erotic element, so also the complexity, the ambiguity, and the paradoxes we find in the representations of the Unicorn may explain the inclination of artists and poets to look for an analogy between the Unicorn and the human.

There is another mythical creature with human or half-human appearance: the mermaid. Interestingly, the same authors who wrote about the Unicorn also wrote about it (or, rather, she): Bishop Theobald in his *Metrical Bestiary*; Bartholomeus Angelicus; Konrad Gesner; Ambroise Paré; Hugo St. Victor; W.B. Yeats, and many others.

Like the Unicorn, the mermaid is represented as half-human, half-mythical, and she also appears and disappears according to her relations with men. But, differing from the Unicorn, she has never had, so far as I know, any divine character or role.

Can we say why or how the Unicorn acquired his unique character among all mythical creatures? In order to answer this question (if it really has an answer), we might better search for the various realms of the Unicorn's representations throughout the ages: their history, their metamorphoses.

1. Thibaut de Champagne, *Poesie du roi de Navarre* II, Les chansons de Thibaut de Champagne, XXXIV. *Bestiaries du Moyen Age* (Paris: Stock, 1980) 121-122.

2. Quoted by Jürgen Werinhard Einhorn, *Spiritalis Unicornis* (Munich: Fink, 1976) 138. Mine is a free translation.

3. The *Mahabharata* III: *The Book of the Forest*, trans. and ed. J. A. B. Buitenen (Chicago: Chicago UP, 1981) 432-447.

4. Mahabharata, 433.

5. Mahabharata, 435.

6. Mahabharata, 436.

7. Mahabharata, 436.

8. Mahabharata, 437.

9. Mahabharata, 439.

10. See Wendy Doniger O'Flaherty, *Siva: The Erotic Ascetic* (New York: Oxford UP, 1973), Chapter II, 42-52.

11. *The Nalinkka Jataka* V, 526, trans. H. T. Francis (London: Luzak, 1969) 79-84.

12. *Nalinkka Jataka*, 82.

13. Quoted in the introduction to Book III of the *Mahabharata*, 191.

14. Samuel Beal, *Romantic Legend of Sakya Buddhism* (London: 1875) 124.

15. J.P. Land, *Anecdota Syriaca* IV (Jerusalem: Biblioteca Syro-Palaestinensis, 1971) 146.

16. Philippe de Thaon, "The Unicorn," trans. Richard Beaumont in *Lyrics of the Middle Ages* (New York: Grove, 1959) 63-64.

17. Guillaume, Clerc de Normandie, *Le Bestiaire Divin*, trans. George Claridge Druce (Ashford: Kent, 1936) 235*ff.*

18. Richard de Fournival, "Le Bestiaire Divin," *Bestiaires du Moyen Age*, ed. Gabriel Bianciotto (Paris: Stock, 1980) 144-145. My translation.

19. Wolfram von Eschenbach, *Parzifal*, Book IX, 482, 27-30; 483, 11 (Berlin: Reimer, 1879) 232. My translation.

20. *Parzifal*, XII, 613: 22-28, 289. My translation.

21. *Le Romans de la Dame à la Lycorne et du Beau Chevalier au Lyon*, ed. Friedrich Gennrich, Gesellschaft für Romantische Literatur 18 (Dresden: 1908) 166-173.

22. Achim von Arnim and Clemens Brentano, *Des Knaben Wunderhorn* (Berlin: Rütten, 1966) 44-45. My translation.

23. Quoted in Einhorn, 143.

24. Pierre de Beauvais, *Bestiaries du Moyen Age* (Paris: Stock, 1980) 38-39. My translation.

25. Quoted in Richard Ettinghausen, *The Unicorn, Studies in Muslim Iconography* I, 3 (Washington, DC: Freer Gallery, 1950) 60.

26. Ettinghausen, 60-61.

27. François Rabelais, *Gargantua and Patagruel*, V, 30, trans. Jacques le Clerq (New York: Modern Library, 1944) 795-796.

28. Aubrey Beardsley, *The Story of Venus and Tannhäuser, or "Under the Hill"* (London: Academy, 1974) 63-64.

29. Quoted in Rüdiger Robert Beer, *Unicorn, Myth, and Reality*, trans. Charles M. Stern (New York: Mason, 1977) 15.

30. Quoted in Beer, 213 *n*148.

Divine Yet Human

Looking at the Unicorn, reading about him, I've found him the most human of all mythical creatures—a projection of human imagination, desires, fears, conflicts, onto a mythical being.

Yet, simultaneously, the Unicorn is represented in art and literature as one of the most divine creatures, whether being conceived by God or perceived as a descendent of God, or an allegory or symbol of God, his might and will.

This combination of the human and divine can provide us one clue to his myth, to the motivations that created this myth. At the same time, and by the same token, this combination poses the most enigmatic and unresolved questions about the birth and growth of the Unicorn's myth and its representations.

The divine character of the Unicorn was represented, according to scholars, in the ancient Persian holy scriptures.[1] In one of them we read:

> We worship the Good Mind and the spirits of the Saints and that sacred beast the Unicorn which stands in Vouru-Kasha, and we sacrifice to that sea of Vouru-Kasha where he stands.[2]

This Unicorn is a three-legged ass who sits amid the sea Varkash and purifies the water. According to the Zoroastrian scriptures, the Unicorn is one of the purest and most sacred animals of Ormuzd, and his mission is to fight the impure animals of Ahriman. About him we read in another holy scripture, the *Bundahish*:

> Of the three-legged ass it is said that it stands in the middle of the ocean and that three is the number of its hooves and six the number of its mouths and two the number of its ears and one the number of

its horns. Its coat is white, its food is spiritual, and its whole being is righteous. And two of its eyes are in the place where eyes should be and two on the crown of its head and two in its forehead; through the keenness of its six eyes it triumphs and destroys.

Of its nine mouths, three are placed in the face and three in the forehead and three on the inside of its loins. . . .Each hoof, laid on the ground, covers the space of a flock of a thousand sheep, and under each of its spurs up to a thousand horsemen can maneuver. As to its ears they overshadow . . . Mazanderan. Its horn is as of gold and is hollow, and from it a thousand branchlets have grown. With this horn will it bring down and scatter all the machinations of the wicked.[3]

This Persian Unicorn is purely supernatural, symbolic and celestial. It is hard to see if and how he is related to the human-divine Unicorn, or to any "natural" animal. But there is in the ancient Persian mythology another Unicorn, called the Koresek, that dwells upon remote hills and takes his pleasure there.[4] This Unicorn resembles some other Unicorns—Chinese, Indian, European—in his fate and behavior. Like other Unicorns, he is brought to the king's palace. Of one Koresek we read that it reared a Zend king and taught him the letters, as the first Chinese Unicorn had taught the Emperor Fu Hsi. Like the Indian Unicorn, the Koresek also was responsible for the good rain and fought against evil creatures.

I don't know if there is any evidence about the relation of the divine three-legged ass and the Koresek. Their myths might have grown in different spheres of culture and religion. But if they were not related to each other in the ancient Persian mythology, they certainly found their way to each other in later times, or in different cultures. The divine aspect of the Unicorn and the human one were always associated in the myth, though not necessarily united. Often we can see the two aspects opposing each other, tending to be separated and yet approaching each other again.

The whole myth of the Unicorn, then, can be read as a story of the complex relationship between the divine and the human as recreated by the artistic imagination. It seems as if the horn itself serves as the bridge between the divine and the human, or between the ways they were conceived in art and poetry. In *Siva: The Erotic Ascetic*, Wendy D. O'Flaherty pointed out the analogy between the god Siva and the human-Unicorn Rsyasrnga. Both of them swing between sexual desires and ascetic commitments. Both dess Parvati or a courtesan—and their sexual activity is meant to strengthen their ascetic chastity.

Siva himself is horned, ithyphallic, but his horns indicate his double character: the ascetic with sexual powers who is fertile. He, like Rsyasrnga, is the great Brahmacarin, the student who has undertaken the vow of chastity, but also the lingam-bearer, who spills his seed upon the earth. And Rsyasrnga is born from the seed of Vibhandaka, spilt upon water when he saw the aspara, herself the daughter of the god or his emissary.

Thus the erect phallus is the sign of priapism but also the symbol of chastity. In some reliefs we see Parvati, the desired wife of Siva, touching his erect phallus as the maiden in many Christian paintings, drawings, and reliefs touches the horn of the Unicorn. But this gesture, or even the erected phallus or horn, indicates more than erotic desire. It is also a symbol of chastity or an act of rejecting eros; it is meant, according to Indian mythology, to break the pride of the god and to remind him of his carnal nature—just as is told in the stories about the human-Unicorn.

After his experience with a woman, the ascetic god, like the human-Unicorn, must be free to return to ascetic life. Moreover, the princess or goddess comes to the ascetic god, or to the human-Unicorn, at the command of her father—whether a god or a king—to avoid a curse of drought, and after that she adopts asceticism with her lover.

The return of the ascetic-god or human-Unicorn to his asceticism is not always simple or easily achieved. In one version of the story about Rsyasrnga, for instance, we read that after he was seduced by Santa, his magic powers vanished and he began to make love to other women. Santa, jealous of the other women, hit him on the head with a shoe, and Rsyasrnga thought: "Why should I, who would not brook the thunder of the clouds, allow a woman to make nought of me?" And he returned to his *tapas*."5

In any case, the resemblance between the human-Unicorn and the ascetic-erotic god is clearly and distinctly asserted. Siva appears in his anti-erotic form, in order to defend the "holy woman" against the seducing demon—but the demon may be Siva himself, and the "holy woman" might be a temptress, or prostitute, yet sent to him by a god. On the other hand, the Yogin, or the human-Unicorn, becomes as strong and as beautiful as a god, and women desire him—probably *because* he is taboo and refrains from being seen by humans—but he must preserve his chastity. In one of the stories, Narada predicts: "Your daughter, O king, is greatly endowed; her husband will certainly be an unconquered hero, like Siva, the conqueror of Kama [the demon]."6

The chastity of the human-Unicorn, like that of Siva, is his way to immortality. But he cannot gain his immortality without passing first through the temptation of eros, the encounter with demons-of-life and with death. The erotic encounter with the woman is itself a kind of death, literal or symbolic, but it is a necessary passage to divine immortality.

In a later version of the analogy between the Unicorn and god, we read that Buddha resolved to devote his final earthly pilgrimage to the salvation of man, and entered the womb of a woman to accomplish that. Thus he might have been embodied in the hermit-Unicorn. For the Buddhists, the Unicorn may have had a purely symbolic significance: the symbol of a quiet, powerful spirit, inclined to solitude.[7] But there is no doubt that the Buddhist versions carried on the more ancient Indian myths, where the analogy or relationship (or both) between the divine and the Unicorn is distinct and direct.

When we turn to the Christian-European myth of the Unicorn, we find again the complex analogies and conflicting relations between the divine aspects and the human ones, though not always in the same direct and explicit representations as in the Indian myths. At the beginning, at least, it seems that the myth of the divine Unicorn is based mainly on an allegorical interpretation of the Old Testament, or rather, its translation by the Septuagint. The earliest source of this myth, the *Physiologus*, which tells us about hunting the Unicorn with the lure of a seducing maiden (quoted in Chapter One), starts the tale in one version by saying: "But my horn shalt thou exalt like the horn of an Unicorn" (Psalms 92:10).[8]

Then comes the story about the hunt of the Unicorn and his being taken to the king's palace. The story ends with the allegorical moral:

> Likewise the Lord Christ has raised up for us a horn of salvation in the midst of Jerusalem, in the house of God, by the intercession of the Mother of God, a virgin pure, chaste, full of mercy, immaculate, inviolate.[9]

In a later version of the *Physiologus* we read:

> In this way Our Lord Jesus Christ, the spiritual Unicorn, descended into the womb of the Virgin and through her took on human flesh. He was captured by the Jews and condemned to die on the cross.

Concerning him, David says: "But my horn shalt thou exalt like the horn of an Unicorn." And Zacharias says, "He hath raised up a horn of salvation for us in the house of his servant David" (Luke 1:69). Moreover, the one horn that he has on his head signifies the words of the savior: "I and my Father are one" (John 10:30). They say that he [the Unicorn] is exceedingly fierce, and this means that neither Principalities nor Powers nor Thrones, nor Angels, nor the most subtle devil nor Hell could hold him against his will. Moreover they say that he is a small animal and this is because of the humility [of Christ] in his incarnation; concerning this he said: "Learn of me, for I am weak and lowly in heart" (Matthew 11:29). Only by the wish of the Father did he descend into the womb of the Virgin Mary for our salvation.[10]

We don't know who the anonymous author of the *Physiologus* was, where he lived, or in what language he wrote his book. According to the scholarly research of J.W. Einhorn,[11] there are more than 77 manuscripts of the *Physiologus* in Greek, plus hundreds of translated versions with variations in many languages, and hundreds of illustrated bestiaries more or less based on it. According to several scholars, the earliest version of the *Physiologus* was written in Alexandria in Greek about 200 C.E., or in Caesaria, in Hebrew, at around the same time.

The story of the Unicorn in the *Physiologus* was changed during the following centuries, developed; it assimilated new elements and around the 14th and 15th centuries evolved in literature and visual art into a rich and complicated myth of the Unicorn, Jesus, Mary, and the hunter or hunters. The basic components of the story as told by the author of the *Physiologus*, however, remained more or less the same. In all the later versions, illustrations, paintings and tapestries inspired by the *Physiologus* or its variations, we have the Unicorn itself representing or symbolizing Jesus and his hunt, and the woman representing or symbolizing Mary. In many of the illustrations of the *Physiologus*, as well as in the paintings and legends inspired by it, we also have the king's palace, usually accompanied by the hortus conclusus, and quite often also the hunters themselves, whoever they might be or represent.[*]

Many of the Christian writers about the Unicorn in the Middle Ages followed the allegory of the *Physiologus*. Thus Justinus, in *Dialogus Contra Tryphonum Judaeum*, who saw the horn of the Unicorn as the typifier for the Christian cross;[12] Tertullian in *Adversus Marcionem*, who wrote: "Christ is meant by this [animal]";[13] St. Ambrose, in his commentary to Psalm 43, who wrote, "who has one horn, unless it be the only-begotten Son of God, which has been next to God from the very beginning."[14] Honorius of Augustodunemis, in *Speculum Ecclesiae* (Mirror of the Church), talked not only about the analogy between Jesus and the Unicorn, but also about the connection with the human incarnation of Jesus:

> Christ is represented by this beast, His invincible might by its horn. Just as the animal is taken in the Virgin's lap by the hunters, so is He found in human form by those who love him.[15]

In a poem by Heinrich von Laufenberg (1390-1460), we read:

> *Der einhürn hüt gevangen ist*
> *in mägden schos mit grossem list,*
> *der ist gewesen jhesus crist,*
> *die maget du, maria, bist. . .*

---

[*]I will return later to these themes of the holy hunt and the hortus conclusus.

53

[The unicorn, it's just been caught
In maiden's lap by cunning thought,
And it was Jesus Christ!
Thou, O Mary, art the maiden....][16]

Einhorn, in his *Spiritualis Unicornis*, devoted full chapters to the Christian writings, which more or less followed the *Physiologus*, or the stories attributed to it, from which I've chosen only a few examples. In most of them we find attempts to explain the difficulties or paradoxes of the alleged original versions. Each in his own way tried to solve simultaneously two problems: the paradox of the incarnation, on the one hand, and the paradox of the analogy between Christ and the Unicorn, on the other.

One of the most illuminating of these attempts we find in the writings of Albertus Magnus (13th century), the important theologian of the medieval period. In *De animalibus libri*, XXVI, 1258 C.E., he wrote:

> The Unicorn is Christ whose might, typified by its horn, is irresistible. The psalm tells us he [Jesus] is as beloved as the offspring of Unicorns; of which Numbers 23:22 also states that his joyousness is as the joyousness of the Unicorn. Jewish Unicorns, particularly faithful to the law, were the ascendants of Mary and her son, the only-begotten son of God. This Unicorn appeared wild and unruly when, at the mere thought of Lucifer's arrogance, it drove Adam out of the Garden of Eden for biting the apple, and destroyed the original world with the flood. Thus also did it destroy the Sodomites with hellfire and brimstone. Thus did that Unicorn rampage in heaven and on earth until our glorious Virgin accepted it into her lap when it entered her citadel, that is to say, into the womb of her chaste body, so that she could nurse it in her bosom and drape

it with the modest flesh, wherein in accordance with the divine decree the unseizable creature might be captured by its hunters, namely by Jews and Gentiles, and yield voluntarily to death by crucifixion. Thus Christ died from the rage he felt against the sinners.[17]

Albertus Magnus's words do not eliminate the paradox, but rather emphasize it. And indeed, the *Physiologus* version of the story about the Unicorn raises many unsolvable questions. Some of them are theological and have preoccupied the minds of Christian theologians of all generations as well as caused controversy, rivalry, and bitter battles: If Jesus was a god, one with his Father, how and why did he become a human being, separated from his Father, born to a virgin? Posing this question, I don't intend to deal with the philosophical-theological-moral ramifications of the double nature of Jesus, as a god and man simultaneously or subsequently. My interest here is in the ways, forms, and patterns of associating the image of Jesus with that of the Unicorn. In other words, how are the high-level theological issues represented in the artistic manifestations of the Unicorn myth?

Another kind of question raised by the *Physiologus* deals with the legend of the Unicorn animal: how and why this fierce and isolated creature let itself be caught—and often killed—by hunters, while we are told that "neither Principalities nor even Angels can hold him against his will." And we may add here another question, more historical: What were the sources that the author or the *Physiologus* drew from or was influenced by?

The third kind of question may perhaps be regarded as a conjuncture of the first two: How and why did the Unicorn become representative of or analogous to the myth of the divine incarnated in the human, of the human transcending of the divine? In other words, why did the author of the *Physiologus* (and, later on, all the hundreds of theologians, narrators, artists, even so-called zoologians, who followed him) need the Unicorn in order to speak about the divine-human Jesus? Or was it the other way around, and the myth of the Unicorn itself—no matter how it became known to the author of the *Physiologus*—inspired him to find the analogy between this exotic and mysterious creature and the divine-human Jesus?

Some of these questions, I'm sure, will remain unresolved. We simply don't have the evidence needed to answer them. Some of them may have been the motivation for all kinds of speculations begotten by intellectual vanity or ignorance. What we do have are not the answers to the theoretical questions but a vast treasure of art and poetry that either has the mark of the story in the *Physiologus* or else has evolved from sources related to it, and, as such, lets us follow the way a wild imagination grows and is shaped as a myth.

We assume, for instance, that the earliest anonymous author of the *Physiologus* lived in a center of Hellenistic culture which at that time was absorbing a flux of various currents coming from many sources of myths, legends and religious symbols. He could have known or heard the stories (Indian, Persian) about the mysterious, secluded creature endowed with divine qualities or missions. He could have known the Zoroastrian myth, or its metamorphosis through the Mithraic and Gnostic myths about the divine one-horned beast that was destined to fight and conquer the evil powers and creatures of the world, or purify the world from evil, sins, and death. He could have seen, or heard about, certain reliefs and mural decorations on the pyramids of Memphis, where a one-horned animal is sacrificed to Isis.[*]

But probably the main source of the story—the combination of the tale about the Unicorn and the

---

[*]Some scholars had rightly pointed out the common elements in the myth of Isis and the traits attributed to the Virgin Mary.

symbolism of Jesus—was the inclination toward allegorism so dominant in the Hellenistic-Christian culture of the first centuries after Jesus. According to this tradition, everything in the world should be interpreted as an allegory of the hidden meaning of the divine realm. This trend probably started with the interpretations of the Jewish Bible made by the Jewish-Alexandrian philosopher Philo in the last century B.C.E., and in quite a natural process was continued by the Christian-Hellenistic interpreters of the Old Testament. Nowadays we tend to dismiss allegorical interpretations of the Bible as naive and irrelevant. But if we read them carefully, we may discover that beneath them, in many cases, lies an ancient myth—suppressed by the official authors of the Bible, but being kept alive and revived by its metamorphosis into the allegory.

In this context of allegorism we may understand how the horn mentioned in the Old Testament became one of the most common sources of motivation for seeing the horn as a symbol of Jesus Christ. It was already a symbol or emblem of strength when called the Horn of David, but it also included the ingredients of a universal myth about redemption and the symbolism of the Messiah. Thus we read in I Samuel 2:10: "And he shall give strength unto his king, and exalt the horn of his anointed."* Or Psalm 132:17: "There will I make the horn of David to bud." Or Psalm 18:3: "My buckler, and the horn of my salvation." And Psalm 89:25: "And in my name shall his horn be exalted." And so on, in other scriptures. The horn, then, is a symbol of might, exaltation, redemption. It is also the symbol of fighting and conquering the evil enemies. It alludes also to a mysterious creature, to the ray of light, to dignity, glory, profusion.[18]

I don't know why the Septuagint translated the word *re'em* as *monokeros* (*unicornis* in the Vulgate); but by doing so, they made it possible to attribute the

---

*In Hebrew the word *messiah* (*mashiach*) is derived from the word *anointed* (*mashuach*).

qualities of the symbolic horns to the mythical Unicorn. Hence, since Jesus was endowed with the virtues of the horn, it's not hard to understand why he was symbolically identified with the Unicorn, according to the allegorical interpretations of the Old Testament.

The allegory of the horn itself, as a symbol of redemption and unity with God, converged with the myth of the one-horned creature. Myth and allegory were thus united into a new symbolical myth. In the early *Physiologus*, the relation between the story of the Unicorn—his description, the tale of his holy hunt, and his allegorical meaning as Jesus—is rather frail and artificial. Yet it does include several hints that would intrigue and fertilize the imaginations of many later creators and interpreters of the divine-human Unicorn. We may assume that the vague hints left vast spaces open for the mythopoeic imagination. Some of them were filled up with free interpretations of the hints and some of them were enriched by other myths or sources of inspiration that could be related to the original text by association, speculation, and fantasy.

Thus, for example, the mere description of the Unicorn as both strong and weak inspired painters, sculptors, poets, to elaborate on this contradiction, and it's hard to tell what preceded or caused what: were the stories about the Unicorn associated with the stories about Jesus, as referred to in the scriptures or their interpretations; or did the ambiguous nature of Jesus, the paradoxes related to his life, influence the ways the Unicorn was represented in stories, poems, paintings? Were the hunters who chased the Unicorn his malignant enemies or were they emissaries of God's will, intended to bring him to the "king's palace," as happened to Jesus himself? And what then is the meaning of the king's palace; what will happen to the Unicorn once he is brought there? What is the relation of the "maiden" to the king's palace, and how could she be imagined and interpreted as the Holy Virgin?

In some of the writings that followed the *Physiologus*, we may find an elaborated attempt to answer these questions in a comprehensive way that would apply both to Jesus and the Unicorn. But in most of the literary and visual art works, the answers given to the questions mentioned above are not theological or theoretical. Rather, they show how a certain myth is developed, expands, uses hints from here and there, assimilates all kinds of sources, yet does not lose the main thread of the original myths that identify the Unicorn with the divine, though never discards his human character.

Again, it may be true about other myths or mythical creatures, but the Unicorn is probably the *primus inter pares* in this combination of divine and human. Some combinations in the verbal or visual myth seem very strange, even weird, in the integrating of images and symbols that appear to be very different from each other, or even antagonistic.

If we bear in mind the needs that urge people to create myth, and the function of mythopoea in poetry and art, the combination of these different elements is not so astonishing and bizarre. The Unicorn himself, his fate, his behavior—though a fruit of the imagination—enabled poets and artists to represent a kind of divine being who at the same time could be very human and yet not be described as such, and who could keep his secret's significance. On the other hand, they could represent an equivocal image of the human being while leaving a space for fantasies that enabled them to endow him with superhuman qualities.

By using the Unicorn as a symbol of Jesus, they could give a freely imaginary interpretation to the fate of a god incarnated as a human. By making Jesus represent some imaginary, spiritual Unicorn, they were free to attribute human qualities to God without having to do it explicitly: they used the mythical animal instead of a human figure. They could also use words or images referring to love, sex, birth and death that would apply both to the human and to the divine without ignoring the differences and tensions between them.

"This wonderful beast," we read in *Le Bestiaire Divin* by Guillaume le Clerc, "which has one horn on its head, signifies our Lord, Jesus Christ, our savior. He is the spiritual unicorn, who took up in the Virgin his abode, who is so especially worthy. In her he assumed his human form, in which he appeared to the world. His people of the Jews relieved him not, but spied on him and then took him and bound him, before Pilate they led him, and there condemned him to death."[19]

Also, according to the mystic Konrad von Megenberg (1309-1374), "Christ, like the Unicorn, was captured by the wicked hunters and by them shamefully put to death. [But] the Unicorn rose again and went heavenward, to the Palace of the heavenly King."[20]

According to Konrad, Christ is also the Unicorn because "before becoming man, he harbored wrath and fury against the vanity of the angels and against the stubbornness of the people on earth."[21]

The hunt for the Unicorn, which is one of the main themes in his myths, is conceived, then, not only as a physical hunt—although it does appear as such in many paintings and drawings—but also as a phase of transition from the earthly existence of the Unicorn to his spiritual and divine one, and vice versa. Between the animal that is hunted and captured and the spiritual Unicorn that is Jesus, we have the image of the human Unicorn, who *wants* to be captured, either because of sexual attraction to the maiden or because he longs for his mother.

> *Unfetter'd by the world at rest,*
> *Peaceful on the mother's breast.*
> *By his artless trust betrayed,*
> *In the trap her bosom made,*
> *Such is the Unicorn's arrest!*[22]

This transition is expressed even more clearly

by Honorius of Autem (1035-1106) in *Speculum Ecclesiae*:

> The Unicorn is a very fierce beast with only one horn. To capture it a virgin maid is placed in the field. The Unicorn approaches her, and resting in her lap, is so taken. By the beast Christ is figured, by the horn his insuperable strength. Resting in the womb of a virgin, he was taken by the hunters, that is, he was found in human form by those who loved him.[23]

Much later, Uhland rewrote one of the *Volkslieder* about the hunt of the Unicorn:

> *A huntsman will a-hunting go,*
> *He's starting from the throne of Heav'n.*
> *What's this encounter'd on the way?*
> *Mary the Virgin, 'tis indeed.*
> *The huntsman whom I mean,*
> *To us is known his fame.*
> *With an angel goes he hunting;*
> *Gabriel's his very name.*
> *The angel blows his tiny horn,*
> *Ev'ry note is well in place;*
> *Greeting to thee, O Mary,*
> *For thou are full of grace.*
>
> *In thy child, thy father's hid,*
> *Thy mother and thy nurse are same,*
> *The Unicorn and now the kid,*
> *Both of them hath she made tame.*[24]

The Unicorn, in this context of the hunt, is conceived sometimes as a symbol of Christ ("Were this Unicorn for us not born, / Then all we sinners'd be forlorn," we read in a medieval song)[25], sometimes as a mystical phenomenon that is incarnated in Jesus through the "womb of the virgin," sometimes as a mysterious creature who wants to be captured so he'll be revealed to humankind in his true, divine-human image. By this conflux of the divine and the human, the whole theme of the hunt was opened to different, even opposing representations.

Was the hunt a "holy hunt" and were the hunters holy too, serving the sacred incarnation of the Unicorn Jesus? Or were the hunters the wicked evils? Was the king's palace a sacred haven for the Unicorn, or his jail, or the place of his assassination? In the Christmas carol of Heinrich von Laufenberg (1390-1460), we read that the dogs hunting the Unicorn were allegories of virtues: "Fröade," "Wille," "Tröstem," "Staete" and "Triawe" (Happiness, Inclination, Consolation, Majesty, Hope). In some mystical poems, the Unicorn is compared to man seeking his salvation and finding it in Mary's bosom; therefore, the hunters are conceived as the emissaries of God. In the visual images of the hunt, there is always a mixture, if not comparison, of the different meanings of the hunt itself, or of the hunters. In a fresco in the Dom of Erfurt (c. 1420), for instance, which is one of the earliest paintings of the holy hunt, it is written explicitly that the hunter is the Archangel Gabriel, and the whole scene of this fresco is clearly meant to accentuate the divine character of the Unicorn. The virgin sits in the hortus conclusus; the chase was not in order to slay the Unicorn, but to drive him into the virgin's bosom; the hounds are the symbols for Christian virtues: Truth, Righteousness, Placidity and Compassion (from the first epistle of St. Paul to the Corinthians 1: 13).

The same is true of a fresco in the Frauenkirche in Memmingen (c. 1460-1470) or in a tapestry from around 1500, now in the Bavarian National Museum in Munich, where the hunter is called Gabriel; or an altar tapestry (c. 1480) where the dogs themselves bear the names of sacred virtues. Again, in an antependium from the 15th century in Gelnhausen, the hunter is called the Archangel Gabriel, who blesses Mary: "Ave Maria, gratia plena. . . ." Thus the hunt of the Unicorn becomes a holy hunt and accentuates the relation between the Unicorn and Jesus.

But the symbolisms of the hunt—if they really should be perceived as symbols—are not always clear and unequivocal. More often, I believe, the hunt is a combination of many aspects of the Unicorn, and derives from different sources, some of them holy and some of them secular. One might see in the famous tapestries at the Cloisters in New York a profusion of religious symbols, either Christian or pre-Christian.[26] But the hunters themselves, the dogs, the scenes of the hunt, are not necessarily related to the holy hunt, and the Unicorn, too, is not a symbol of Jesus, although one may try to interpret him as such. These tapestries represent a fantastic, beautiful, probably mysterious animal that somehow invaded "realistic" scenes of a hunt, referring more to a typical historical background of hunting than to a sacred one.

Yet it may be that these late tapestries are an illuminating example of the long and complex assimilation of different motives and images in one work of art. In a fresco by Falconetto (1514), in the Church of St. Pietro Martire, Verona, we can detect the same ambiguity about the meaning of the hunt. Mary is sitting inside the hortus conclusus near the king's palace, holding the Unicorn in her lap. (The Unicorn here has the body of a lamb—a clear allusion to Jesus—but with a bent horn.) On the left side of the conclusus we see the angel—presumably Gabriel—with the hounds. On the right side is a Roman soldier with a sword, also chasing the Unicorn. And again in a Franconian tapestry (c. 1450) now in the Bavarian National Museum in Munich, the hunter is in the damsel's (Mary's) lap. The hunter here represents lust—the Unicorn, pure love.

Looking further at illustrations of the *Physiologus*, the bestiaries, or the psalters, we find in some of them the same ambiguity about the character of the hunters: they may appear as wild hunters chasing the pure Unicorn—but also as the lovers of the maiden, probably jealous of the Unicorn; they are the wicked Roman soldiers, who chased Jesus, and the angels who drove him into Mary's bosom; they are also the wicked heretic Jews, but actually they perform a sacred mission; the Son of God, we read, was transformed into a Unicorn, and was hunted through the forests of this world in order to be brought back to the palace of the king, which is heaven.[27]

In a similar way, the idea, or theme, is demonstrated by a medieval German folk song included in Ludwig Uhland's *Alte hoch-und-neiderdeutsche Volkslieder*:

> *I stood in the Maytime meadows*
> *By roses circled round,*
> *Where many a fragile blossom*
> *Was bright upon the ground;*
>
> *And as though the roses called them*
> *And their wild hearts understood,*
> *The little birds were singing*
> *In the shadows of the wood.*
>
> *The nightingale among them*
> *Sang sweet and loud and long,*
> *Until a greater voice than hers*
> *Rang out above her song.*
> *For suddenly between the crags,*
> *Along a narrow vale,*
> *The echoes of a hunting horn*
> *Came clear along the gale.*
>
> *The hunter stood beside me*
> *Who blew that mighty horn,*
> *I saw that he was hunting*
> *The noble Unicorn—*
>
> *But the Unicorn is noble;*
> *He keeps him safe and high*
> *Upon a narrow path and steep*
> *Climbing to the sky;*
> *And there no man can take him;*

He scorns the hunter's dart,
And only a virgin's magic power
Shall tame his haughty heart.

What would be now the state of us,
But for this Unicorn,
And what be the fate of us,
Poor sinners, lost, forlorn?
Oh, may He lead us on and up,
Unworthy though we be,
Into his Father's kingdom
To dwell eternally.[28]

In most of the stories, poems, frescoes and tapestries about the holy hunt (which was not always holy), we have another component that unites the divine and human characters of the Unicorn and the maiden, and this is the hortus conclusus, which quite often is identified with the king's palace or is related to it either by verbal interpretation or by visual description, as an annex to the garden or as surrounded by it. Here too we have a fascinating and strange mixture of different sources, allegories, influences.

We may start again with the story of Rsyasrnga in the Mahabharata, where the courtesan sent to seduce him designed a hermitage, "prettily wooded with artificial trees of various blossoms and fruits."[29] After she succeeded in seducing him, she enticed him into her retreat, wherefrom he was taken to the king's palace and married to his daughter. Whether the legend of Rsyasrnga reached the Hellenistic Near East or not, it's interesting to notice that the human-Unicorn is taken to the king's palace through an enchanted hermitage, which is in a way a replica of the secluded garden-hermitage where he lived before being seduced.

In the *Physiologus* story, as we've seen, the Unicorn is captured and brought to the king's palace with the collaboration of the tempting maiden. Here too, as in most of the following scenes of the hunt for the Unicorn as told and painted in many centuries,

the background of the hunt and the capture of the
Unicorn is either in a secluded forest or meadow, or,
more explicitly, the hortus conclusus. I believe that
in order to understand the role of the enclosed garden in the myth of the Unicorn, we should turn to the
allegorical interpretation of the Song of Songs.

This interpretation started in the first centuries of
the Common Era (both by Christians and by Jews,
although for different purposes) and was developed
later on into a complete allegorical myth. The allegory of the enclosed garden is only one component of
the myth, but it may serve as an important clue to
the whole treasure of symbols that grew from an allegorical approach. Many Biblical scholars and his-
torians of mythology have pointed out the paganistic
and mythical sources of the Song of Songs (the Song
of Solomon in the Authorized Version). They have
traced the dramatic elements of this love poem back
to the Sumerian, Assyrian, Phoenician rites of love
among gods, and the paganistic-erotic meaning of
the apple, the pomegranate, the garden of nuts.[30]

In my opinion, too, the later allegorical interpretation of the Song of Songs manifests the ways in
which an ancient myth is transformed into a religious allegory and then transformed again into a
new myth. What we certainly have are several elements that later on, during medieval times, were assimilated into the myth of the Unicorn, when the
Christian allegory itself became a renewed myth. It
was a long process of development, through elaborations of the original themes, through assimilating
other myths and absorbing them as parts of the
whole story, through transforming several elements
of the Song of Songs into components of the love and
hunt of the Unicorn and the Virgin.

The first component of the allegory of the Song of
Songs is the king's palace itself, whereto the "hero-
ine"—the maiden, the bride—is brought. "Draw me,
we will run after thee: the King hath brought me into
his chambers: we will be glad and rejoice in thee . . ."
(Song of Songs 1:4). This theme is repeated several

times in the song: the maiden is brought to the palace to enjoy the king's love. In the allegory, the king is God himself, and the maiden is Mary, according to the Christians, or the Shechina, according to the Jews.

In addition to the king, there is another lover in the Song of Songs, who does not dwell in the palace, but "he comes leaping upon the mountains, skipping upon the hills . . . [and] is like a roe or a young hart. Behold he standeth behind our wall. He looketh forth at the windows . . ." (2:8-9).

Several passages in the Song of Songs accentuate the theme of forbidden or unachievable love between the "dove" and the "roe." She is seeking him, and cannot find him (3:1). He is coming secretly to her, but disappears: "I sleep, but my heart waketh: it is the voice of my beloved that knocketh, saying, Open to me, my sister, my love, my dove, my undefiled. . . . I rose up and opened to my beloved . . . but my beloved had withdrawn himself, and was gone; I . . . sought him, but I could not find him; I called him, but he gave me no answer. . . . I charge you, O daughters of Jerusalem, if ye find my beloved, that ye tell him that I am sick of love" (5:2-8).

These and similar verses of the Song of Songs were the source of inspiration and imitation for many love poems, both in the Chivalric poetry of the late medieval era and, later, in Romantic poetry. They were also the source of inspiration for mystic poetry based on the religious allegory of the Song of Songs.

There are in the Song of Songs several different direct or indirect answers to the question of why the lovers could not consummate their love. One of them is that the maiden, or virgin, was not yet prepared for this love. Many verses and metaphors affirm this concept. For instance, when the maiden charges the daughters of Jerusalem "that ye stir not up, nor awake my love, till he pleases" (2:7; 8:4). Or when it is said about her, "We have a little sister, and she has no breasts: what shall we do for our sister in the day when she shall be spoken for?" (8:8). And other verses that allude to her youth and presumed virginity.

The other reason given for the unconsummated love is the fact that she had already been taken to the king, and thus cannot find her lover or he cannot approach her. Her brothers, we are told, "made me the keeper of the vineyards; but mine own vineyard have I not kept" (1:6). The maiden, then, is a captive in the king's palace, and her lover cannot reach her. "Behold his bed, which is Solomon's; three score valiant men are about it. They all hold swords . . ." (3:7-8). In the eyes of her lover, she is as "terrible as an army with banners" (6:4) or a door that her brothers will "inclose . . . with boards of cedar" (8:9).

But there is in the Song of Songs another image that became the main source of inspiration for poets and artists when they told or painted the love of the maiden and the Unicorn. In Chapter 4, after the Bridegroom (or, rather, the forbidden lover) praises the beauty of his love and calls her to come with him "from Lebanon . . . from the top of Shenir and Hermon, from the lion's dens" (4:8),[*] and after he tells her that "thou hast ravished my heart, my sister, my spouse. . . . How much better is thy love than wine! and the smell of thine ointments than all spices" (4:9-11), he says almost with a sigh of confession, admitting the unachievable love: "A garden inclosed is my sister, my spouse; a spring shut up, a fountain sealed. Thy plants are an orchard of pomegranates . . . with all trees of frankincense. . . . A fountain of gardens, a well of living waters, and streams from Lebanon." (4:12-15) This is the most living image of the ambiguous love between the "dove" and the "roe," and the most inspiring one: the enclosed garden is the place where all the enchanting, fruitful powers of sexual desire and love are growing and flowing: the pomegranate, the pleasant fruits, the myrrh and spices, the well of living waters. But it is a "spring shut up, a fountain sealed." The bride asks, or prays:

---

[*]These names of the mountains allude to the seclusion of the lover's original dwelling and also to his divine origin.

Awake, O north wind; and come, thou
south; blow upon my garden, that the
spices thereof may flow out. Let my
beloved come into his garden, and eat his
pleasant fruits. (4:16)

She tells the "daughters of Jerusalem" that her
beloved "is gone down into his garden, to the beds of
spices, to feed in the gardens, and to gather lilies"
(6:2). And the lover has already told her:

I am come into my garden, my sister,
my spouse: I have gathered my myrrh
with my spice; I have eaten my honeycomb
with my honey; I have drunk my wine
with my milk . . . (5:1).

And again:

I went down into the garden of nuts to
see the fruits of the valley, and to see
whether the vine flourished, and the
pomegranates budded. (6:11)

Reading the Song of Songs without any attempt to
allegorize or interpret, we know that this wonderful
encounter of the lovers will remain only wishful
thinking, or desire. He will look for her, tell her that
"the winter is past, the rain is over. . . . The flowers
appear on the earth; . . . and the vines with the ten-
der grape give a good smell" (2:11-13). Therefore he
will ask her, "Arise, my love, my fair one, and come
away" (2:13). She will say:

Let us get up early to the vineyards; let
us see if the vine flourish, whether the ten-
der grape appear, and the pomegranates
bud forth: there will I give thee my loves.
The mandrakes give a smell, and at our
gates are all manner of pleasant fruits,
new and old, which I have laid up for thee,
O my beloved. (7:12-13)

Love, we hear:

> . . . is strong as death, jealousy is cruel
> as the grave; the coals thereof are coals of
> fire, which hath a most vehement flame.
> Many waters cannot quench love, neither
> can the floods drown it. . . . (8:6,7)

Yet in spite of this powerful love, she remains a garden enclosed, surrounded by walls and boards of cedar, and all she can do is to repeat her calls-of-love, to ask him to set her "as a seal upon thine heart," and to pray, "Make haste, my beloved, and be thou like to a roe or to a young hart upon the mountains of spices" (8:14).

Whether we read the Song of Songs as a myth of love among gods, or as a poetic drama of "romantic" love, the elements of a genuine myth are always there. Some of the metaphors in the passages praising his or her beauty sound like conventional similes. But most of the metaphors grow from the alive and intense drama of the quest for love and its unachievability. Thus, her being an "inclosed garden," and his being compared to a wandering, almost mysterious stag are neither conventional topoi nor artifices. They do include the connotations of some inner, profound unity between natural forces and human desires; between attraction and taboo; between the unapproachable, adorable beauty and the natural, naive love of the shepherd.

No wonder, then, that the Song of Songs inspired so many allegorical elaborations of love, or the renewal of myth through mysticism. The "inclosed garden" itself was a source of inspiration. The comparison of woman, or maiden, to an enclosed garden, or a fountain sealed, should not be understood as a simile for virginity only. It also has the connotation of the profound secrecy of womanhood, of her ambiguous role as the living waters, the orchard of pomegranates (a symbol of fertility), and the forbidden garden, the hidden or sealed fountain of the forces of life. One does not have to be Christian (which I am not) in order to understand the inclination to perceive the enclosed garden as the "divine feminine." The Jewish mystics did the same when they wrote about the Song of Songs and identified the garden with Shechina, the female-god, whether or not they were influenced by the Christian symbolism. Simon Magnus, the Gnostic of the 1st century C.E., interpreted the garden as the "womb of the world," whether he'd read the Song of Songs or gotten the interpretation from some Persian—Zoroastrian or Mithraic—source.[31]

We know, of course, that the Song of Songs was a vast treasure of inspiration, association, and directly or indirectly related representations, through medieval art and poetry. It is not hard to see how a connection was made between the images—transformed into symbols—of the Song of Songs and similar legends about the Unicorn and the "immaculate inviolate" virgin. The main feature that linked them, as I have said previously, was the image of the enclosed garden, associated with the king's palace.

It might be that the author of the *Physiologus* based his analogy of the king's palace and the enclosed garden a Christian allegorical reading of the Song of Songs, or that he got it from a Mithraic source, where the word *paradise* itself (*pairidayza* in Persian) means wall-of-clay surrounding a garden—that is, a combination of palace and garden.[32] In any case, the symbolic connotations of the virgin-mother and the garden-palace (both open, fruitful, and closed, protected by walls) are already present. The hortus conclusus itself, then, is a combination of poetic imagination about human love, a renewal of myth, and an allegorical or mystical interpretation of the garden-palace, connoting its divine character or meaning.

But how was the Unicorn interwoven into this mythical-allegorical scene? In the Song of Songs the lover is compared to a roe, or a young hart—an antique and common simile for the handsome young lover. How and why was the hart (or stag, or roe) transformed into a Unicorn? I can only speculate. It might be that the author of the *Physiologus* heard some stories about the Unicorn and the maiden, though I don't know any proof that the Indian story of the human-Unicorn and the maiden was known in the Hellenistic world in the 3rd or 4th centuries. It might be that the author of the *Physiologus* already knew the allegorical comparison or metaphor of Jesus and a horned creature and connected it with the symbolic interpretation of the Song of Songs. But the hart of the Song of Songs did not suit the symbol of the sacred creature and his relation to the mother-virgin in the king's palace. The hart itself was a familiar, too well-known animal. For the rich and mythical texture of the story, one needed a more mysterious creature, born more of fantasy and more divine than the earthly hart. (Although there are some poems and paintings where Christ is likened to a stag: "Her son was drawn / As deer is torn / In chase" or "By this stag we rightly understood Jesus Christ.")[33] Thus was the Unicorn "invented"—with or without the influence of other sources—as the suitable substitute for the hart in the Song of Songs: a creature that had already—according to the Septuagint and the Christian interpretation of the horn—the qualities needed for such a divine being and its incarnation as the hunted lover.

Whether my speculation is right or wrong, there is no doubt that the later verbal and visual representations of the hortus conclusus, certainly a symbol borrowed from the Song of Songs, and its relation to the Unicorn, answered the needs of connecting the mythical garden-palace with a divine yet human creature. The motif of the hortus conclusus, the Virgin and the Unicorn, was repeated in dozens if not hundreds of paintings, illustrations, tapestries. It specially flourished in the late medieval centuries and the Renaissance, the reasons for which are related to the expansion of Mariology on the one hand and the *Chansons d'Amour* and *Minnerlyrik* in France and Germany in the 12th to the 15th centuries on the other. In all of them we find the combination of the sacred, divine hortus conclusus, which became the natural place for the virgin, or the unachievable maiden—a kind of metamorphosis of the bride in the Song of Songs—and the metaphorical character of the bridegroom as the divine lover, who appears in the image of the Unicorn, symbolizing Jesus.

It is not necessary, of course, always to look for an explicit allegorical or symbolical meaning for the literary and artistic images of the Virgin with the Unicorn in the enclosed garden. The combination of the three elements—the virgin, the garden, and the Unicorn—gained an independent life over the centuries, often represented in the creative imagination of a poet or a painter who found the motif itself rich and inspiring, and who probably did not think at all about the metaphorical or allegorical meanings. Yet we cannot ignore the allusions to the mythical sources, since only through them can we grasp the search for the Unicorn himself as a symbol both for human love and a divinely mysterious role and fate.

Moreover, only when we recall the original sources of the Unicorn as divine and human can we understand how and why he became one of the most lively and expressive centers of myth, capable of representing or relating to other and vastly different mythical motifs. In my search for the Unicorn, I have found him standing alone or in the company of other animals or in the company of men and women, in a peaceful kind of paradise, or on a battlefield fighting other animals, sometimes submissive and sometimes aggressive and lustful, a peace-lover or diabolic. The various and contradictory images and icons of the Unicorn are related to the different traditions where they have grown, and to different historical and religious backgrounds. Sometimes they indicate the personal interest of a painter or a poet in this creature. More often, it seems to me, the representations of the Unicorn as a divine creature follow a traditional, conventional iconography, yet leave a space for some variations, though usually we don't know the individual painter or poet who made the variations. We meet the individual artist only in the late medieval period and then in the Renaissance and after.

Both in the conventional and in the more individual representations of the Unicorn, we can trace the permanent vacillation between the human character of the Unicorn and his divine and mythical nature. Quite often it seems that the artist himself could not make up his mind what kind of an animal he was coping with, where did he come from, what were his mission and his fate. The Unicorn was always too beautiful, too supernatural in his appearance and behavior to be regarded as a simple "natural" creature. On the other hand, he always manifested some character—good or evil—that made him similar to a human being. I believe that this conflict, or ambiguity, was one of the main sources of inspiration for many of the artists and poets who represented him in their works.

I've found this antagonism, or ambiguous combination, even as late as the poetry of Rilke. In *The Notebooks of Malte Laurids Brigge*, Malte is leading Abelone in the Musée Cluny, to show her the tapestries of the Lady and the Unicorn, and it is clear that these tapestries, and the Unicorn himself, served as an inspiration for Malte's dreams about love.[34]

But in *The Life of the Virgin Mary*, we read:

> *Oh, if we only knew how pure she was!*
> *Did not a doe, that resting, once espied*
> *her in the woods so lose herself in looking*
> *that in her, without pairing, the unicorn*
> *begot itself, the animal of light, the creature*
> *   pure. . . .*[35]

Here, and in some of the letters Rilke wrote later, the Unicorn is clearly a divine creature; and the same is true about his poem *The Unicorn*, in *New Poems* (1907):

The saint looked up, and his prayer
fell back like a helmet from his head;
for the never-believed-in silently approached;
the white animal, that like an abducted
helpless hind beseeched him with its eyes. . . .[36]

In the sonnet to Orpheus (quoted in the Prologue), the Unicorn is a creature "invented" by artists, and may combine both the divine and the human characters of this animal "that never was." Rilke's different—if not to say opposing—attitudes to the Unicorn are in a way the summing up of similar attitudes during the whole long history of the Unicorn, of the Unicorn-in-art-and-poetry.

1. Shepard, 233-240.

2. *Yasna* XLIII, 4, *Sacred Books of the East* XXXI, 291; quoted in Shepard, 235.

3. Quoted by Borges, *The Book of Imaginary Beings*, 35-36.

4. *Bundahis* XIV; see Shepard, 238.

5. O'Flaherty, 49.

6. O'Flaherty, 56.

7. O'Flaherty, 49.

8. Einhorn, *Spiritalis Unicornis*, 274. Einhorn quotes the Vulgate, Psalm 91:11; I have quoted the Authorized Version, Psalm 92:10.

9. Shepard, 49.

10. Quoted by Margaret B. Freeman, *The Unicorn Tapestries* (New York: Dutton, 1976), 19. A similar version can be found in Pierre de Beauvais, *Bestiaire*, 38-39. There are dozens of books referring to or quoting the anonymous *Physiologus*; they differ in details but not in content and spirit.

11. Einhorn, 50-81, quotes Sbordone's three editions of the *Physiologus* as well as Erik Peterson's ediition, and others. There is no single authentic book of *Physiologus*, and it is not clear exactly when the books was written or whether there ever was one original *Physiologus*.

12. Einhorn, 49. My translation.

13. Einhorn, 49. My translation.

14. Einhorn, 201. My translation.

15. Beer, *Unicorn*, 79.

16. Einhorn, 201.

17. Albertus Magnus, *De Animalibus Libri*, trans.

James J. Scanlon, Medieval and Renaissance Texts and Studies (Binghamton, NY, 1987) 180-181.

18. For various metaphors of the horn in the Hebrew Bible, see, for example, Exodus 34, Deuteronomy 35, I Samuel 2, Habakuk 3, Psalms 18, 89, 112, Ezra 29. In all these examples, and in many others, the horn symbolizes light, glory, might, dignity, magnitude, profusion.

19. Guillaume, 44-45. In many cases, authors refer to the Unicorn as "him" or "he," not "it."

20. Otto Keller, *Die Antike Tierwelt*; trans. in Freeman, *Unicorn Tapestries*, 25.

21. Freeman, 25.

22. From a missal at Neuhausen, Germany; Beer, 98.

23. Honorius of Autem, *Speculum Ecclesiae* in Freeman, 25.

24. Ludwig Uhland, *Alte hoch-und-niederdentsche Volkslieder* in Beer, 104.

25. Beer, 105.

26. The religious motives in these tapestries are dealt with in detail by Freeman as well as by John Williamson, *The Oak King, The Holy King, and the Unicorn* (New York: Harper, 1986).

27. The same idea is repeated in various versions by Konrad von Megenberg, Guillaume le Clerc, Johannes a San Geminiano, Rudolph von Ems, and many others. For a full and detailed list, see Einhorn, 137-167.

28. Uhland, *Volkslieder* in Shepard, 82-83.

29. *Mahabharata*, 434.

30. See, for instance, Theodor H. Gaster, *Thespis* (New York: Anchor, 1961). Williamson's *The Oak King* follows similar arguments.

31. See F.E. and F.P. Manuel, "History of Paradise," *Myth, Symbol and Culture*, ed. C.G. Geerz (New York: Norton, 1974) 98.

32. See Leroy A. Campbell, *Mythraic Iconography and Ideology* (London: Brill, 1908), 129-130.

33. Philip de Thaon, *Bestiaries*; quoted in Freeman, 73. Also see Saint Basil, Homily 13, *Exegetic Homilies*, trans. Sister Agnes Clare Way (Washington, D.C.: Catholic U of America P, 1963) 207-208.

34. Rainer Maria Rilke, *The Notebooks of Malte Laurids Brigge*, trans. M.D. Harter Norton (New York: Norton, 1964) 111-113.

35. Rainer Maria Rilke, "The Annunciation," *The Life of Mary*, trans. Albert E. Flemming (New York: Methuen, 1986) 128-129.

36. Rainer Maria Rilke, "The Unicorn," *New Poems*, trans. Edward Snow (San Francisco: North Point, 1984) 77.

The Creature From Paradise
With a Hundred Faces

1. Adam, Eve and the Unicorn

In a Flemish tapestry from the beginning of the 16th century, now in the Galleria Accademia in Florence, Adam is giving "names to all cattle, and to the fowl of the air, and to every beast of the field" (Genesis 2:20). As could be expected, one of these "beasts of the field" is the Unicorn; moreover, he strides foremost, before the lions, the elephant, the giraffe, very proud, as if he is really "prime among peers."

Mythical or "real," the Unicorn is in paradise among other beasts and animals but somehow superior to them. Thus we see him with Adam and Eve in the house altar of Herzoz Albrechts V in Munich, the closest animal to Eve; in the *Paradiesbild* by Lucas Cranach the elder (now in the State Museum of Art, Dresden), the Unicorn appears with a group of other animals, but above them, closer to Eve; in the Catherine Chapel in Siena, in a mosaic-on-marble on one of the floors, Adam is sitting in Paradise, apparently talking to the animals, holding a mirror. The same motif of the Unicorn in paradise appears in countless numbers of works of art and poetry.

It seems, then, that when artists began to illustrate the Bible, especially Genesis and the Psalms, they included the Unicorn, whether or not they believed that such a creature existed. The fascinating story about paradise, and more so about paradise lost, invited the fascinating image of the Unicorn, as a paradigm for paradisiac creatures. (In his *Spiritalis Unicornis* J.W. Einhorn includes a detailed list of the illustrated Bibles from the second half of the 11th century on, where the Unicorn appears among other animals that God created and assigned to Adam for naming.)[1]

Those artists, we should remember, already knew some bestiaries where the Unicorn was described or illuminated, such as the bestiaries that followed the *Physiologus* or the *Originum sive etymologiarum lib-*

ri XX of Isidore of Seville (c. 560-636 C.E.).

But the Unicorn was not just *one* of the animals in paradise. From the earliest illustrations of the Bible, he had a unique place and role. When God matched Adam and Eve in paradise, in a 15th-century miniature by Bartholemeus Anglicus, the animal closest to them was the Unicorn. In an illustration in a Dutch Bible, 1440, where Adam is naming the animals, the first that he named was the Unicorn.

In a tapestry in Basel from the 15th century we read, above the head of the paradisiac Unicorn, *Got muss al geschäffen han* (God certainly created all things), as if the artist himself wondered whether God created even the unique, mysterious Unicorn. A similar, earlier theme is to be seen in the 11th-century tapestry of creation in the Cathedral of Gerona. In the right central section Adam is naming the animals, among them the Unicorn.

The inspiration for the paradisiac Unicorn was linked not only to the Bible. In certain illustrations of Ovid, and in paintings related to Ovid's *Metamorphoses* XI, we see Orpheus in a paradisiac environment, playing to the animals the first animal of which is the Unicorn. This theme of Orpheus and the Unicorn was repeated in many etchings and paintings,[2] and it might be related not only to Paradise but also to the idea of resurrection associated with some legends about Orpheus.

What happened to the paradisiac Unicorn after the expulsion of Adam and Eve from paradise, when paradise was lost? Other animals, we know, remained upon the earth, were saved from the flood in Noah's ark and are still to be seen. But the Unicorn disappeared; or, if not, he had to be found in a new context, in a new myth.

What we really face here is a challenge to the creative imagination—poetic, artistic—that was either motivated by two main exponents of the myth of the Unicorn or was derived from two sources of this myth. The first is the mystery of the disappearance of a creature that, according to legends or stories told

Adam Giving Names to the Animals (tapestry, Galleria Accademia, Florence)

by witnesses, as it were, had once existed some-where. How can he be forced to reappear or how can he be caught? The second source or motivation is the nature of the Unicorn as a divine-and-human crea-ture, namely, a creature endowed with the potential for reincarnation in different forms and qualities.

Both of these sources or challenges are related to each other and interact upon each other, and it is im-possible to say which came first, which begot the oth-er. It is obvious that they nourished one another, were interwoven in complex textures that may be in-terpreted as belonging to either of them or to both. We should not look for a logical sequence or a chrono-logical order of the different stories about the para-disiac Unicorn after paradise was lost or barred to humans. The legends, the allusions and commen-taries are confused, exchanging places and se-quences, replacing each other. After paradise, the paradisiac Unicorn was lost or barred, but he may appear in hundreds of different forms and tales. In many of them it seems as if the Unicorn himself has become the focus of the myth of the lost paradise and the fate of the human race after the loss.

We may even rewrite the history of the Unicorn from his first appearance in paradise on, although not in the chronological order of his representation in books and visual arts. Many early events of this history were told or painted much later than others that appear in earlier books and paintings. In some of the paintings, tapestries, books we find a combi-nation of many or all of the elements of the recon-struction of this history.

Reconstructing the history of the Unicorn from paradise on, I was not at all surprised to find him participating in the first sin of Adam and Eve. He certainly belonged there. Thus, in a c. 1500 Swiss tapestry of paradise, we see Adam and Eve after the sin, with a Unicorn lying down between them and above the words *Adam Wo Bist Du?* ("Adam, . . . where art thou?" Genesis 3:9) The question might re-fer not only to Adam but to the Unicorn as well.

Lucas Cranach the Elder, *Paradiesbild* (painting, Staatliche Kunstsammlungen, Dresden)

The role of the Unicorn as a participant in the scene of the first sin has fascinated the imaginations of poets and artists in different ways. One of them was to perceive the Unicorn himself as the tempting devil—a metaphoric serpent or its associate in seducing Eve. We should not be surprised: from its earliest representation in Indian myth, the Unicorn was both the holy creature and the sinner. Christian myth accented this double-faced nature or at least hinted at it in many ways; and, naturally, it referred to the paradisiac Unicorn: he already contained the potential for being or developing both his holy and his unholy, devilish character. In his homily on Psalm 28, Saint Basil had written:

> But, when it is necessary to take vengeance and to overthrow the power attacking the race of men, a certain wild and savage force, then He will be called the son of Unicorns.

> For as we have learned in Job, the Unicorn is a creature irresistible in might and unsubjected to man. . . .

> It has been observed that the Scripture has used the comparison of the Unicorn in both ways, at one time in praise, at another in censure.

> "Deliver," he says, "my soul from the sword . . . and my lowness from the horns of Unicorns" (Psalm 21:21,22). It seems that on account of the promptness of the animal in repelling attacks it is frequently found representing the baser things, and because of its high horn and freedom it is assigned to represent the better.

> On the whole, since it is possible to find the "horn" used by Scripture instead of "glory" . . . or also, since the "horn" is fre-

Adam and the Unicorn (mosaic, St. Catherine
Chapel, Siena)

quently used instead of "power" . . . Christ
is the power of God; therefore, He is called
the Unicorn on the ground that He has one
horn—that is, one common power with the
Father.[3]

Thus, in a Tintoretto fresco (San Rocco, Venice), in
a scene of Eve giving Adam the famous apple, the
third participant (truly quite hidden and hardly
seen, as befits him) is not the serpent but the Unicorn. And Tintoretto's fresco is only one among many
similar scenes.

This motif of the Unicorn's involvement in the first
sin or even of his representing the serpent-devil itself attracted not only the imagination of poets and
artists but also the speculation of Christian theologians. For some of them, it is related to the allegorism of Jesus as the Second Adam. (We find a similar motive in the play *Mystère d'Adam*, from the
16th century.) For some of them, it was rooted in the
artistic imagination that substituted for the shape of
the snake that of the horn and attributed to both the
role of sexual seduction. Or it might have been an
imaginary analogy between the serpent-and-Eve story and the story of Unicorn and the maiden.

I once saw such an analogy in a humorous relief
above the door of a tavern in Erfurt, which was called
the *Goldenes Einhorn*. In the center of the relief we
see a maiden embracing a Unicorn, while on the left
side are Eve and the seducing serpent. Curiously
enough, this tavern stands across the street from the
Erfurt Cathedral (c. 1420), where the scene of the
Virgin and the Unicorn is one of the most holy among
those in this iconographical category. In this cathedral's fresco, too, Eve appears, but not as a sinner or
seducer or the seduced; rather, as a repentant
woman kneeling at a garden fence—the garden
might be paradise or the hortus conclusus—seem-
ingly in adoration of the Unicorn.

This confusion or interchange between the serpent-devil and the Unicorn was repeated quite often

in the Middle Ages, in various contexts. In some of them, as I mentioned earlier, Jesus was the second Adam and Mary the second Eve. In many cases the confusion or analogy can be traced back to the mythical beginnings of the story of paradise. Both theologians and artists have found there, in the imaginary paradisiac creature, the source for a complex elaboration of the relation between the holy and the diabolical, as well as between death and resurrection.

The myth of the Unicorn in paradise, before the Fall and afterward, posed many questions and many challenges for all those who were attracted to it throughout the ages. For instance, they asked themselves what happened to the Unicorn after the Fall. Where, in what form, role, or place had the Unicorn existed after paradise? Was he doomed to die or disappear, and, if so, whereto did he retreat or how could he reappear and resurrect?

In an early version of the story about the death of the Unicorn, we read in the Talmud that "the first bull that Adam sacrificed to God [after the expulsion from paradise] had one horn on his brow."[4] Does this mean that there was only one Unicorn, and that after he was sacrificed there were no more? We don't find the myth of the Unicorn in the post-biblical Jewish literature. (Jews probably were careful not to let this myth invade their imaginations, because of its connotations for Christians, who considered one horn more sanctified than two, indicating the unity of the world with God.) Yet, in several passages in the Talmud, we read about the Tahash (or, in other passages, the Keresh), an animal with one horn on its brow; and it was eventually encountered by Moses, who used its skin for building the tabernacle. After that, it was concealed.[5] The term *concealed* in Jewish sources often means that what is concealed will reappear one day, like other primordial beings or entities—the primal light, for instance. Moreover, we read in the same passage that since this animal that Adam sacrificed is said to have had one horn, it is unblemished (kosher), suitable for sacrifice. And

Rabbi Jehudah added: "The bull that Adam sacrificed had one horn on its brow, therefore he was purer than other animals, since it is said (Psalms 69:31), 'This also shall please the Lord better than an ox or bullock that hath hooves.'" Whatever animal the Talmudic sages may have meant, it is clear that this one-horned ox or bullock was pure and that it is concealed somewhere, probably until the primeval days of paradise return.

This motif, which is only hinted at in the Talmud, is abundant in many legends about the Unicorn, whether or not they are connected to the Judeo-Christian Paradise. The Unicorn, then, is a "paradisiac" creature, hidden there or in some substitute for paradise, maintaining his purity (although very often containing a non-pure potential), his innocence, his holiness (although very often mixed with diabolic inclinations).

In most of the myths of the Unicorn, at the beginning of his history, he lives in a kind of paradise full of primeval trees, fountains, balsams and does not wish to get out of this enclosed and secluded place. In an Arabian book, I've found the most extreme metaphor of the Unicorn's refusal to leave his paradise. The young Karkadan—an Arabic version of the name of the Unicorn—puts its head out of its mother's womb before it is born and then retreats there after it has looked around, apparently having glimpsed a human creature.[6]

In the various legends about Noah's ark, we are told or can see that the Unicorn was too big to enter the ark and therefore was left alone in the water; and we don't know if he survived the flood or was drowned and later resurrected. In some tales, the Unicorn was too proud to be saved by Noah and claimed that he would experience death alone. Another reason given for the belief that the Unicorn was not saved in Noah's ark is based on Scriptures, according to which Noah was ordered by God, "And of every living thing of all flesh, two of every sort shalt thou bring into the ark, to keep them alive with thee;

they shall be male and female." (Genesis 6:19) Since the Unicorn was alone, without a mate, Noah could not take him.

The same motifs were repeated in many later tales and illustrations. In a woodcut by Tobias Stimmer (1576), the Unicorn refuses to board Noah's ark. In a poem, *The Unicorn and the Ark*, published in 1975, the Unicorn refuses to enter the ark and tells Noah, "I don't believe in the concept of death."[7] Somehow the same motif transmigrated to Polish and Ukrainian tales about the Unicorn who refused to enter the ark, saying that he could swim, but the birds who reposed on his horn drowned him. Thus the Unicorn was either extinguished by the flood and miraculously resurrected or appeared again somewhere.

In any case, the Unicorn did not want to go out of his paradisiac shelter, either because he couldn't protect himself against temptations or because he had some destination, some role he had to follow and fulfill. But he did go out, after all.

What happened to him afterward?

There seems to be no limit to the boisterous behavior of the legendary Unicorn, or rather, to the frenzy of the imagination of the poets and artists referring to him. Yet there is some inner logic or consequence in the ambiguity, the double-faced character of his representations as a post-paradise being. In all of them, we may trace the permanent conflict between the divine and the human, the holy and the diabolical, the wildly bestial and the spiritual, that men saw in this mysterious creature.

2. *Fierce and Mild, Vain and Meek, Cruel and Kind*

From the earliest descriptions of the Unicorn, both in writing and in visual arts, we find the antagonistic face and shape of the Unicorn, whether alone or in association with other animals or men. According to Megasthenes (c. 175-255 C.E.), the Unicorn (called Cartazoon) is wild, aggressive, and only mild in the rutting season, when with his mate; afterward he again becomes unsociable and wild.

Julius Solinus wrote in his *Polyhistoria*:

> But the cruellest [of all animals] is the
> Unicorne, a monster that belloweth horri-
> bly, bodied like a horse, footed like an ele-
> phant, and headed like a stag. His horn
> sticketh out of the midst of his forehead . .
> . so sharp, that whatsoever he pusheth at,
> he striketh it through easily. He is never
> caught alive; killed he may be, but taken
> he cannot be. . . .[8]

Again, in the 7th-century *Origenes* XII by Isidore
of Seville we read:

> Rynoceros in Greek is so meanynge an
> Horne in the nose, and Monoceros is an
> Unycorne: and is a right cruel beast. . . .
> And his horn is so sharp and so strong that
> he can fight even the elephant and kill
> him. He is so strong that he is not taken
> with might of hunters. . . .[9]

Scholars have pointed out that the stories about
the Unicorn were sometimes mingled with the descriptions and legends about the Indian rhinoceros.
And it is true, as Richard Ettinghausen remarks,
that in the books about the Karkadan or the Kharish
(also called Shadhavar, Kartazon, Karduum,
Krakuzan, Khartut, Sinad) of Al-Damiri, Al-Tawhidi, Al-Dazwin, and others, from the 10th to the 13th
centuries, it is hard to tell if they refer to the rhinoceros or to the legendary Unicorn. But even in the
stories attached to the rhinoceros, it is stunning to
find how gentle and beautiful this ugly beast could
become, while it is also described as being fierce, aggressive, hostile to men.

Al-Damiri, for instance, tells us that the Karkadan "is very hostile to man. When it smells him or
hears his voice, it pursues him, and after having
reached him, he kills him."[10] But according to Al-

Tawhidi, the Kharish "is a certain small animal of the size of a kid or lamb, and very quiet—but it has such strength of body and swiftness of motion, as to baffle a hunter. . . . Nothing can subdue it."[11] And here Al-Tawhidi repeats the story of the stratagem for seizing the Karish by exposing it to a young virgin. Whether he derived this story from the versions of the *Physiologus* or from the Indian sources, it is clear that no real rhinoceros known from nature could be imagined as sucking the breasts of a young virgin or fainting—as Al-Damiri wrote—from her odor. We face here, too, the legendary double-faced Unicorn: small and gentle, fierce and aggressive.

Moreover, we read in Al-Qaziwini that on its (the Shadhavar's) single horn are said to be 42 hollow branches that form a kind of Aeolian flute, because the wind produces cheerful sounds when passing through them. These are so pleasant that other animals are attracted to it. The same story, with certain variations, was told by Jabir b. Haiyan and Al-Damiri. (It appears in an illustration to a Persian manuscript from the 14th century.)[12]

In other stories, the Karkadan is described as letting a dove rest on his horn, while he peacefully enjoys its cooing. And again in a book attributed to Al-Qaziwini, the Karkadan has a tremendous horn from which jut out fourteen short branches, projecting in alternate directions. All these descriptions and illustrations certainly do not apply to the rhinoceros; they are parts of the myth about the legendary Unicorn, who plays tenfold roles, opposing yet complementing one another.

Somehow, the differences or the antagonistic characters of the Unicorn did not prevent poets and artists from attributing them to the same creature. From early reliefs, illustrations, and stories, we may conclude that the Unicorn was a monster, fighting against all other animals—both the peaceful elephant and the fierce lion—and also against man. Yet he remained the most peaceful, benign, helpful, meek animal on earth.

The most peculiar aspect of this phenomenon is demonstrated by the fact that those artists and poets and even so-called scholars who wrote about it or illustrated stories about it apparently accepted the tenfold contradictory images and tales about the same creature. For instance, we find a Unicorn represented as a rhinoceros on the pavement of St. Mark's in Venice, near the Door of the Madonna, and may wonder what it is doing there. Perhaps the artist himself confused the two creatures, or else he may have followed a long tradition, not of merely confusing but of blending the image of the monstrous animal with that of a holy, beautiful one. (Artists may also have been confused by the Vulgate's translating *Re'em* as either *Unicorn* or *rhinoceros*.) When he returned from India where he had seen the rhinoceros, Marco Polo believed that he had seen the Unicorn, although he recorded that it "is not in the least like that which our stories tell of as being caught in the lap of a virgin; in fact, 'tis altogether different from what we fancied."[13] Yet in the *Livre des merveilles*'s illustrations to Marco Polo's book (c. 1351 C.E.), we see a beautiful, proud Unicorn resembling a young horse, with one horn, leaping near an imaginary mountain. He certainly could be attracted by a young girl or attract her.

In many of the psalters, the bestiaries, the illustrations to the *Physiologus*, the Unicorn is drawn as an ugly monster, quite often resembling the heavy rhinoceros or some other one-horned beast, even while flirting with a maiden or kneeling before a motherly figure. In other illustrations—sometimes in the same book—he is drawn as a humble kid or a beautiful, proud horse. In the *Roman d'Alexandre*, Alexander is fighting against one-horned dragons and snakes, but he himself is riding on Bucephalus, his famous horse, which in some miniatures has one horn on his brow.

In an *Alexanderlied* written by Pfaffen Lamprecht in the 12th century, we read about the gifts sent by Queen Candace to Alexander the Great, among

The Unicorn as Rhinoceros (mosaic, St. Mark's, Venice)

which was a "beast of proud and noble mien, that
bears in his brow the ruby-stone"; but later we read
that "no man of woman born endures the terror of his
horn."[14] (According to Ettinghausen, this legend was
probably derived from the Persian *Iskander-Namah*
by Nizani.)[15] Similar stories were written about the
gifts that the Queen of Sheba brought to King
Solomon. From the original story in the Bible (Kings
I 10:2) we know that she brought him "precious
stones," and in the later legends—mostly Arabian or
Persian—the most precious stone was hidden in the
Unicorn's horn.

In *The Temptation of St. Antony*, Flaubert included both aspects of the Unicorn—the good and the
evil. In Scene 2, the Queen of Sheba approaches
Antony and tries to tempt him with her "wedding
presents," among which there is a Unicorn, his
precious horn, and the Simorg-anka, which, according to certain Persian lore, was the transfiguration
of the Unicorn. But in Scene 7, the devil brings to
St. Antony all kinds of monsters, among them the
Unicorn: "My hooves are of ivory, my teeth are of
steel" and "my head is coloured crimson . . . and the
horn on my brow has the motley shades of the rain-
bow. . . ." This unicorn runs so fast that he leaves the
wind behind and can "be bridled only by a virgin."[16]

The horn itself, of course, is the most noticeable
and prominent mark of the Unicorn, and many scholars have dedicated their research to its treasure—its
use, value, and relation, direct as well as indirect, to
the general myth of the Unicorn.[17] The horn, according to some legends, is very heavy, very long,
mighty beyond any natural horn of other animals. In
some legends, the horn is described as being of different colors (black, white, orange), different shapes
(spiral or straight, sharp or thick), and different con-
sistencies (tough or flexible). Some of these descriptions resulted from actual objects that were known
by sight and regarded as true horns of the Unicorn,
although they actually were ivory or the tusks of the
narwhal. Some of the so-called horns were mere

fakes, manufactured by artisans who knew that customers—kings, dukes, bishops—were ready to pay a high price for them, especially during the Renaissance. But there's no doubt that several traits attributed to the horn were related to the legends of the mythical creature; for example, its aphrodisiac powers, its capacity to protect one from enemies, its magical properties as a protection against or cure for poison—all because it is the divine horn, symbolizing Jesus.

One of the links between the merits of the horn as such and the myth of the Unicorn is the story about the precious stone hidden inside the horn. This stone would itself make the Unicorn a target for hunting. But since it was impossible to catch the Unicorn in "natural" ways, the whole story about finding the precious stone became a part of the myth of the Unicorn and his exceptional nature. The quest for the horn was even compared to the quest for the Holy Grail. Thus we read in *Parzifal*:

> *We caught the beast called monocirus,*
> *Who knows and loves a maiden so much*
> *That he falls asleep upon the maiden's breast.*
> *We put the heart of this beast*
> *Upon our ruler's painful wounds.*
> *We took the carbuncle-stone*
> *That sparkled against the beast's skull-bone*
> *From underneath his horn. . . .*[18]

The precious stone of the Unicorn could be found only by killing him and cutting his horn away, but the horn itself is known, or reported, as a healing lifesavior, which is one of the ways that the horn became a prominent part of the myth.

In the Greek version of the *Physiologus*, we read the following story about the magical power of the horn:

> There is a great lake in those regions,
> where the animals congregate for drink-

ing. However, before they assemble, the serpent approaches and spits her venom into the water. The animals detect the poison and dare not drink but await the arrival of the Unicorn. Up he comes, goes straight into the water and makes the sign of the cross with his horn. This detoxifies the water, and then all the other animals too can drink.[19]

The sources of this belief in the power of the horn may be pre-Christian, but the allegorical interpretation of the horn as a symbol of the cross enabled the later stories about the horn to become an integral part of the myth of the Unicorn as a symbol of Jesus. The lake was then called the "Waters of Life," polluted by the serpent / devil and purified by the horn of the Unicorn representing the cross.

But we read a similar story about the rhinoceros in a book of voyages by Linschoeten:

> . . . by the River Ganges in the Kingdome of Bengala are many of these Rhinoceros, which when they will drinke the other beasts stand and waite upon them, til the Rhinoceros hath drinke and thrust their horne into the water . . . and then after him all the other beasts doe drinke. Their hornes in India are much esteemed and used against all venime, poyson, and many other diseases. . . .[20]

Is it probable, then, that the rhinoceros is the source of all the marvelous qualities attributed to the Unicorn and his horn?

The confusion between these two animals was very common and repeated in hundreds of translations, descriptions, diaries, works of art. Quite often one cannot really tell whether a manuscript that mentions the Unicorn was written about the rhinoceros or vice versa. Sometimes we read a so-called eyewitness testimony about the rhinoceros and wonder if it is not just a plagiarism of the legends about the Unicorn. We read, for instance, a description of the rhinoceros that purges the water of poison in *Among the Mountains in High Ethiopia* by Marmol Caravial (c. 1575), and it seems to be another version of the European legends about the Unicorn's horn, but located in exotic Ethiopia and pretending to be based on fact. The description records that the horn of the rhinoceros is used against poison because the animals are known to wait until the rhinoceros dips his horn to purge the waters before they drink. I doubt that this was a deliberate fraud. The writer himself might have confused the two animals or, rather, the legends about them, as so many other writers had.

Another example of confusion or plagiarism is the story about the hunting of the rhinoceros told by Fray Luis, also about Ethiopia. There we read that

> When they learn that one is near at hand they load their muskets and they take a female monkey which they have trained for this kind of hunting, and they bring her to the place. She begins at once to run about looking for the rhinoceros, and when she sees him she leaps here and there and dances as she goes toward him, playing a thousand monkey-tricks. He is much delighted in watching this entertainment, so that she is able to approach until she can throw one leg over his back. Then she begins scratching and rubbing his hide, and this gives him keen pleasure. At last, jumping to the ground again, she starts to rub his belly, and then the rhinoceros is so overcome with ecstasy that he stretches himself out at length upon the ground. At this point the hunters, who have been hidden all the while in some safe place, come up with their cross-bows or muskets and shoot him.[21]

The story itself belongs to a series of legends about the marvelous court of the Emperor Prester John, who ruled Ethiopia for more than 500 years and sent his letters—in Hebrew!—to the popes and kings of Europe. The Unicorns play a prominent role in those legends and alleged letters. Quite possibly the stories about the rhinoceros are descendants of the Unicorn myth, but they certainly add to the confusion between the Unicorn and the rhinoceros.

The legends about the healing and purifying powers of the Unicorn's horn were repeated numberless times. Many of them were deliberately created in order to increase the commercial value of the horn, whether faked or taken from the narwhal or various animals. Other legends are directly related to the allegory of Jesus-as-Unicorn: the horn is the symbol of the Cross and, as such, it has the power to purify water.

But this power is mentioned earlier than the Christian allegorism. As we've seen, the Persian Unicorn—the three-legged ass—is said or, rather, asked by prayer, to purify the water of the venom of Ahriman and his evil creatures, among which the serpents are the most prominent and dangerous. The same role of the Unicorn as a healer or purgative can be found in other non-Christian legends. The Indian story about Rsyasrnga, who caused the rain to fall, may also be related to the myth about the Unicorn as a benign creature, friendly toward other creatures and helping men in their needs. But even the Indian human-Unicorn was transformed in a later Japanese tale into a one-horned demon and appears as a monster in some Chinese icons.[22]

In a Japanese No play from the 16th century C.E., *Ikkaku Sennin*—a metamorphosis of Rsyasrnga—overpowers the Rain-dragons, shuts them up in a cave and maliciously stops the rains from falling for twelve years. Only when a beautiful lady of the court—or Santa, the king's daughter—seduces the one-horned sorcerer, and by cheating him rides on his back to the king's palace, does she rob him of his magic powers, liberate the dragons, and allow rain to pour down.[23]

Following the double-faced character of the Unicorn, we see him and read about him as a warrior beast fighting other animals, sometimes winning and sometimes losing. Guillaume le Clerc wrote in his bestiary: "This beast is so daring, so pugnacious and so bold, that it picks quarrels with the elephant. It is the fiercest beast in the world, of all those that are in it. It fights with the elephant and it wins."[24] But even this strong beast—compared by Guillaume to Jesus—is captured by a maiden or with her help. Does that mean that the Unicorn is still the winner in his fight against his enemies? From most of the stories and illustrations, we have to conclude that the Unicorn is simultaneously strong and weak, fierce in fighting but vulnerable, or willing to submit and to die. Moreover, his weakness and submission are not always the result of his confrontation with the maiden (though in the late medieval period and the Renaissance, it appears to be the main reason). From the earliest stories about his fight against other animals or against man, the Unicorn includes in his nature the traits and behavior of both the fierce winner and the weak loser, whatever the reasons for this double character might be.

In the Indian and Arab legends about the fight of the Unicorn, his usual enemy is the elephant. The sources or inspiration of these legends are probably the stories—whether imaginary or not—about the fight between the elephant and the rhinoceros. In Europe, though, the usual enemy is the lion.

One source of the association between the Unicorn and the lion may be found in Psalms 22:21—a line that was used quite often by the Fathers of the Church and later theologians as an allegorical figure for Jesus: "Save me from the lion's mouth: for thou hast heard me from the horns of the Unicorns."

We have many different translations of this line in English. In one of the earliest, we read: "Save me from the lion's mouth and [save] my humbleness from the horns of the Unicorn." According to this translation, the lion symbolized hell, and the Unicorn symbolized pride and might. The concept of the Unicorn's horn as a symbol of might and pride is supported by several other lines in the Old Testament, and the early Christians referred quite often to another line in the Psalms: "But my horn shalt thou exalt like the horn of an Unicorn. . ." (92:10).

Since the Christian writers relied on the Septuagint translation of the Old Testament, they had to deal with the rivalry of two mighty and proud animals, the lion and the Unicorn, that were related somehow to the tradition of Christ's symbols. On the one hand, we have the blessing of Jacob to Judah in Genesis 49:9, where Jacob said: "Judah is a lion's whelp: from the prey, my son, thou art gone up: he stooped down, he crouched as a lion, and as an old lion; who shall rouse him up?" Judah, as we know, was the ancestor of David, King of Israel, and according to Matthew 1 and Luke 3, he was the forefather of Jesus. Besides, the medieval Christian writers often referred to another line in the Psalms: "There will I make the horn of David to bud: I have ordained a lamp for mine anointed" (132:17). Thus, the Messiah-Christ belonged to the pedigree of David-Judah; that is, he was related directly to the lion. Therefore we read in Philippe de Thaon's bestiary that "The lion signifies the son of St. Mary; he is king of all the people."[25] And according to Bishop Theobald (11th century), "As the lion dwells on the high mountain, so Christ, the spiritual lion, dwells in the highest heaven."[26] And again, Peter Abelard (1079-1112) wrote: "As the young of the lion, so Our Lord is risen . . . on the third day."[27]

On the other hand, we read about Joseph in Moses's blessing to the Children of Israel: "His glory is like the firstling of his bullock, and his horns are like *the horns of Unicorns*; with them he shall push the people together to the ends of the earth . . ." (Deuteronomy 33:17; emphasis added).

Now, throughout the history of Israel during the

period of the First Temple, the tribes of Judah and Joseph were rivals, fearing and fighting each other. Thus symbolically, the two majestic animals, the lion and the Unicorn, were perceived as enemies, yet attached to each other. According to a later, Christian tradition, Jesus was related to both of them: to the lion, king of all the animals, and to the Unicorn, whose horn reached to heaven like the horn of David's house.

There is a Christian adaptation of a Talmudic legend:

> When David was leading his father's sheep in the desert, he saw a Unicorn sleeping and thought it was a hill, and sat on it. Suddenly the Unicorn awakened and started to rise to its feet. David clasped the Unicorn's horn, which reached to heaven, and prayed: Lord of the Universe, lead me to safety and I'll build you a temple one hundred cubits in span, like the horn of this beast. So God sent a lion, king of beasts, before whom the Unicorn crouched in obeisance. Since, however, David was afraid of the lion, God sent a deer for it to pursue, and David then slid down from the Unicorn's shoulder and escaped. On that it was said, "Save me from the lion's mouth; for thou hast heard me from the horns of the unicorn."[28]

In the original Talmudic Midrash we have, of course, the Re'em, not the Unicorn, and it has two horns, not one.[29] Besides, in the original Midrash, David doesn't promise to build a temple "like the horn of this beast"; but from both the original and the adaptation, we may learn about the antiquity of the imaginary confrontation of these two animals, which was repeated many times with significant variations, and with controversies over which of the two animals was superior.

The sources for the legends of the confrontation between the Unicorn and the lion are not necessarily only biblical. They might have been formed in some more ancient representations. One of them, for instance, is a relief on the lid of a toilet-box found at Ur of the Chaldees (the birthplace of Abra-ham), where a lion grips with teeth and claws the hindquarters of a one-horned beast. There may be other reliefs or paintings from antiquity that I don't know but that were known to artists and poets of earlier ages. In any case, the motif itself attracted the attention of scholars and begot many theories and speculations about the specific meaning of the confrontation between these two animals.

One speculation about their rivalry is that they are the emblems of the sun (lion) and the moon (Unicorn) with which they have been connected frequently through the ages. In the *miserere* seat in the parish church at Stratford-on-Avon, I saw the figure of the Unicorn with a crescent moon over its head. Old alchemical charts commonly designate the figure of Luna by placing in her right hand a single horn.[30] Murillo, in his paintings of the Assumption, painted the crescent moon over Mary's head, and it is probably connected with the lore of the Unicorn. According to many astrologers, the moon purifies the air of noxious vapors, which might be compared to the role of the Persian three-legged ass in purifying water and to the similar story about the Unicorn.

In his book about the Unicorn, Robert Brown advocated the lion/sun-Unicorn/moon theory: "The lion-sun flies from the rising Unicorn-moon and hides behind the Tree of the Grove of the Underworld; the Moon pursues and, sinking in her turn, is sun-slain."[31] This hypothesis appealed to many scholars who sought in the myth of the Unicorn traces of some ancient mythology about the cycle of seasons, represented by certain animals and trees. ("If the lion and the Unicorn are to represent the sun and the moon, they will need no less a tree than this 'Tree of the World' as the scene of their encounter.")[32]

I don't believe that one theory or hypothesis can really explain the relationship between the Unicorn and the lion. It seems to me that poets and artists in the late Middle Ages and during the Renaissance were nourished from various sources—most of them foreign or inexplicable—and were combining symbols when they wove elaborate, complex allegories into their pictures and poems.

Whatever the poets and artists meant to do consciously, they have used the confrontation between the lion and the Unicorn as a suitable means for representing the fascinating image of the Unicorn. The lion is the well-known king of beasts; the Unicorn is the "horse-from-heaven," a semi-god, and spiritually superior to all other animals. He is the mysterious Beast-from-Paradise, who was incarnated in the divine-yet-human figure of Jesus. If the Lion represents earthly power, the Unicorn is the superior majestic spiritual beast. Each one of them may be the winner and the loser at the same time, but both are attracted to each other and appeal to the creative imagination.

In Edmund Spenser's *The Faerie Queene*, the Unicorn is the loser:

> *Like as a Lyon whose imperiall powre*
> *A prowd rebellious Vnicorn defyes,*
> *T'avoid the rash assault and wrathfull*
> *   stowre*
> *Of his fiers foe, him to a tree applies,*
> *And when him ronning in full course he*
> *   spyes*
> *He slips aside: the whiles that furious beast*
> *His precious horne, sought of his enemyes,*
> *Strikes in the stocke, ne thence can be*
> *   releast,*
> *But to the mighty victor yields a bounteous*
> *   feast.*[33]

Similar scenes of the Unicorn killed while sticking his horn into a tree were repeated in many illustrations and stories. The fight between the Lion and the Unicorn is also told in Ariosto's *Orlando Furioso* (6: 69; 44: 86) and likewise in other poems, some of which I've yet to find and read. In some of them, the death and the tree have allegorical meaning, indicating the fatal defeat of the spiritual beast when fighting the earthly powers. Some of them pretend to be an "objective" description of the fight between two powerful animals. In Topsell's *Historie of Foure-Footed Beastes*, we read:

> He is an enemy to the Lyons, wherefore as soone as ever a Lyon seeth a Unicorne, he runneth to a tree for succor, that so when the Unicorne maketh force at him, hee may not onley avoide his horne, but also destroy him; for the Unicorne in the swiftness of his course runneth against the tree wherein his sharpe horne sticketh fast, then when the Lyon seeth the Unicorne fastened by the horne without all danger, he falleth upon him and killeth him. These things are reported by the King of Aethiopia, in an Hebrew Epistle unto the Bishop of Rome.[34]

The Unicorn and the lion do not always have to be considered as enemies. In *La Roman de la Dame à la Lycorne et du Biau Chevalier au Lion*, an epic poem from the end of the 13th century, we read about "la dame" and "le biau chevalier" riding on their beasts, the Unicorn and the lion, after the knight has liberated his beloved (pure and chaste) from the castle.[35] But in *L'Astrée*, by Honore d'Urfe (1568-1625), the "Fontaine enchanté de la verité d'amour" (The Enchanting Fountain of the Truth of Love) is first guarded by both lions and Unicorns. Later on, when the lovers recognize their true love and fidelity, they are attacked by the lions, and the Unicorns rush to protect and save them.[36] (The book was illustrated by Augustin de Saint-Aubin [1736-1807], who painted the scene where the lions attack the lovers and the Unicorns rush to defend them.) The allegorical meaning of the novel is clearly expressed: the Unicorn simultaneously symbolizes both love and death.[37]

In two Flemish tapestries in the museum of Count Borromeo (Isola Bella, Lago Maggiore), the battle is not resolved; in one of them, the Unicorn is attacked from behind by the lion and it seems he is the loser. In the second tapestry—I could not tell which comes first chronologically—the Unicorn attacks the lion, stabs him with his horn and is apparently the winner.

In Elieser Susmann's fresco (1735) on the ceiling of a synagogue (now in Museum Israel, Jerusalem), the lion and the Unicorn are fighting, but from the painting itself, it's hard to conclude who will win.

The most famous—and probably the most beautiful—encounter of the Unicorn and the lion is in the six tapestries called *La Dame à la Licorne* (now in the Musée Cluny, Paris). Much has been written about these tapestries: their historical account, their artistic evaluation, and their assumed allegorical meaning— singular or plural.[38] Naturally, most of the interpretations and stories are concerned with the dame: who was she, what story did she represent, what is the hidden meaning of her relationship to the Unicorn, if there is one? As Alain Erlande-Brandenburg has rightly said, we are impressed not only by the mystery of the dame, but also by the history of the tapestries, which is a charming and fascinating thriller, as well as a source for many legends and historian's speculations. Who made these tapestries? For whom? Who or what is represented by the dame—is she a legendary lady from the East, the wife of a king or duke, or the Virgin Mary? None of the many explanations stand up to critical examination, and, in my opinion, it's better to leave the mysteries unresolved and open to all kinds of interpretations and impressions.

Yet in all six tapestries, we see the two rival animals, the Unicorn and the lion, confronting each other, and probably competing for the dame's attention or love. They do not fight any longer. They are enclosed, together with the dame, her maid, and various animals, on an island-carpet, ornamented with flowers, surrounded by trees—two or four—and the whole scene seems to occur in an artificial paradise, beyond battles and worldly desires. The lion himself is, at least in four of the six panels, either ironic or indifferent, as if to say, "All this is behind me." The Unicorn, though more curious—in one or two panels even longing—does not rush to fight the lion. He seems to say, "There is nothing I can do now. I'm a captive, on this isolated island, and the most I can do is to win the dame's touch on my horn, while she herself turns her head away from me." Only in the panel called *Mon Seul Desir* do the lion and the Unicorn show some symptoms of desire, but without real battle or intention to win. I don't know if this panel was meant to be the last one. Probably so, if we accept the interpretation that here the dame puts her jewelry in the box and intends to go away, as if saying that this is the "end-game."

It is quite possible that the Unicorn abandoned his desires and hopes after seeing his image in the mirror. Not accidentally, I think, he does not (and we do not) see his erect horn in the mirror. Does he see the expression on the dame's face, a mixture of compassion and mockery, or of accepting fate? In most of the known paintings of the Unicorn and the maiden, he puts his head on her lap, or his horn beneath her dress. Here it is too late for that, and the lion is still there, watching or mocking.*

In other paintings and stories we see the brave, proud, fighting Unicorn sometimes peacefully offer-

*It seems that the Unicorn and the lion did not have to remain enemies forever. In the coat-of-arms of the kings of Britain, the lion—formerly the emblem of England—and the Unicorn—formerly the emblem of Scotland—hold the crown peacefully together, although they had been enemies, as were England and Scotland

Unicorn Fighting with Lions (tapestry, Museum
Borromeo, Isola Bella)

ing his love to the maiden or mother, sometimes fighting for her love; sometimes letting a Wild Woman ride on his back when he rushes into a battle against wild enemies; sometimes defending himself or the lady against lions, dragons, human enemies. In all cases he remains ambiguous, double-faced, a strange combination of opposing traits and powers.

While I was searching for the Unicorn in Italy and Germany, time and again I was stunned by the different representations of his horn, literal and symbolic. One Unicorn I saw was standing at Isola Bella, atop the private church of Count Borromeo, near his castle. To my taste it was a very kitschy Unicorn: a huge, mid-19th-century sculpture of a horse with one horn on his brow, and a winged demon riding on his back. There were many other Unicorns at Isola Bella. On the balustrades of the balconies in the courtyard and in the park were several iron Unicorns, some of them with broken horns. At the entrance to the castle/museum was an engraving of a Unicorn with wings, quite demonic. I learned later that the Unicorn (in Italian he is called Unicorno, Liocorno, and Licorno) was a part of the coat-of-arms of the Borromeo family, which has owned the island since the 15th century and was meant to be shown with the animal's head raised toward or against the viper, the emblem of the Count Visconti, Borromeo's enemy.

The horns of all these Unicorns (both on the Isola Bella itself and on the fronts and balustrades of some houses in Arona, the neighboring town) were tall and erect, emblems of pride. Yet the word *Humilitas* was engraved near most of them, to accentuate the spiritual character of the creature. Kitsch or not, the juxtaposition of the erect horn and the word *Humilitas* was not accidental and didn't start with Count Borromeo or his artisans. As I realized later, it was a typical manifestation of the ambiguous attitude toward the Unicorn. He was blessed or doomed to be both proud and humble, and the horn was naturally

La Dame à la Licorne, La vue (tapestry, Musée Cluny, Paris)

one means for expressing this combination.

Later I saw a submissive Unicorn in the floor mosaics of the Krypta San Savino in Piacenza, dating from the 11th century. The section with the horn is blurred, but one can still make out the saint blessing the Unicorn, whose horn is bent. In the Duomo of Cremona, again in the floor-mosaics of the krypta, there was a small Unicorn among other animals, including the centaur, with his head bent in *humilitas*. I saw the same representation of a humble Unicorn with his horn bent in the Church of Santa Maria in San Benedetto, near Mantova, in a mosaic from the 11th century. Near the Unicorn, on the floor, were the words *Prudencia, Iustitia, Fortityda, Tempramenta*. And I saw one again in the floor mosaic of San Giovanni Evangelista in Verona, from the 13th century.

It was more difficult for me to decide if the Unicorn in the floor mosaic of the Cathedral of Otranto was submissive or proud. The floor contains twelve circles, and in each one appears a different animal, or monster, or Adam and Eve. But only in one circle do we also see the artist himself, Pantaleone, who worked there for two years (1163-1165) and created the whole mosaic, with the Tree of Life in its center, and many figures—representing Biblical stories, animals, and human figures, allegories, symbols of good and evil. The Unicorn belongs to this magnificent story-in-mosaic, but it is hard to tell how serious the artist-monk was when he diverged from the other themes to represent the Unicorn and the artist together: both of them have a comic expression and their juxtaposition is comic too.

We may of course assume that the image of the humble Unicorn, with his bent horn, was influenced by the Christian concept of Jesus, the meek and humble. But this interpretation does not apply to the whole range of works of art that show how fascinated the artists were when they depicted the double character of the Unicorn through the expression of the horn. The history of iconography is also not suf-

La Dame à la Licorne, Le toucher (tapestry, Musée Cluny, Paris)

The Humble Unicorn (mosaic, krypta of the Duomo, Cremona)

A Unicorn with a Bent Horn (mosaic, Cathedral, Siena)

The Unicorn and the Artist (mosaic, Cathedral, Otranto)

ficient to explain the different constructions of the mysterious horn, which is sometimes bent and sometimes erect and long, or even both in the same book or work of art.

Thus, for instance, the Unicorn's horn is bent when he approaches the maiden—whether she is meant to represent Mary or not—or when he is tamed by her while putting his head in her lap. The horn itself, in many cases, may be the symbol of aggressive desire or of submission, of frivolity or of chastity. For example, in the Maulbroun (Germany) church choir stall, the virgin is probably Mary in an enclosed garden and the Unicorn approaches her with a bent horn. The same image appears on the engraved stone in St. Stefan's Church in Vienna. Sometimes, instead of the chaste virgin—usually Mary—we have a wild woman, and the Unicorn approaching her is fierce, demonic, with an erect horn. In the famous Malterer tapestry (1310-1329), the virgin is taming the Unicorn, but the tapestry comprises several examples of "feminine wiles." The capture of the Unicorn may be one of them; he seems to willingly accept his fate by bending his horn.

It may seem strange that the erect horn of the Unicorn represented chastity, yet many of the paintings showing the Unicorn in this relation are based on Petrarch's sonnet "The Triumph of Chastity." Dozens of illustrations of these works were collected by Eugene Müntz and d'Essling.[39] I've seen only two: one, made by Liberale at the end of the 15th century, is in the Castello Vecchio museum, Verona and is called *The Triumph of Chastity*. We see there a chariot led by two Unicorns with erect horns, and in the chariot a woman, Lucrecia, sits as the symbol of chastity. On the right side of the panel, four horses lead another chariot, inside which there is a lady wounded by arrows, and this work is called "The Triumph of Love." The Unicorns perhaps are meant to represent chastity and the horses infidelity.

In another fresco (1459), by Piero della Francesca, now in the Uffizi, Florence, we have the same theme of "The Triumph of Chastity." In one panel two unicorns lead a chariot, inside which Battista Sforza is sitting, with an angel in front of her. In the other panel two horses lead a chariot, in which her husband, Federico Sforza, is sitting. In both paintings—and in many similar ones—the choice of the Unicorns with erect horns may have been ironic; all the more so since Battista Sforza, as far as I know, was not exactly the paradigm of chastity.

But probably the choice was not ironic. Probably the erect horns were able to serve as demonstration of both sexual desire and chastity. The Unicorn himself, as we have seen, served simultaneously as the symbol of sexual desire and chastity. He embodied both in his posture, his behavior, his ambiguous horn. Even in cases where chastity fights against lust, it is hard to tell the exact role of the Unicorn: does he represent chastity, or lust, or both?

In the famous *Garden of Delights* by Hieronymus Bosch (in the Prado, Madrid), we can see the juxtaposition of the Unicorn's horns in a rich complex of representations. In the upper part of one panel we see Adam and Even naked in paradise and surrounded by animals, among them two Unicorns—one with a straight horn, dipped in water, the other with a bent horn. In the central panel of the triptych, the Unicorn appears at the bottom, carrying a youth on his back and an apple on his horn. In another part of the same panel, the Unicorn appears again with a youth riding on his back, but here the horn is shaped like a tree branch. The whole triptych is based on the polarity between the Garden of Eden (the left panel) with Adam and Eve before the Fall, and Hell (the right panel), with the distorted surrealistic bodies of men and monsters.

The middle panel is dedicated to the Praise of Sin. The Unicorn is seen in all the panels, belongs to all of them, represents innocence and sin, life and death. When we follow him through other paintings and books, we can see how broad and rich are the realms of the polarization.

3. *Divine and diabolic, savior and destroyer, dead and resurrected*

In the Old Testament, the Unicorn is mentioned by that name only in the translation by the Septuagint. But a one-horned animal, playing his ambiguous role, appears in the Apocalypse of Daniel. We read there:

> Then I lifted up mine eyes, and saw, and, behold, there stood before the river a ram which had two horns: and the two horns were high; but one was higher than the other, and the higher came up last.
>
> I saw the ram pushing westward, and northward, and southward; so that no beasts might stand before him, neither was there any that could deliver out of his hand; but he did according to his will, and became great.
>
> And as I was considering, behold, an he goat came from the west on the face of the whole earth, and touched not the ground: and *the goat had a notable horn between his eyes*.
>
> And he came to the ram that had two horns, which I had seen standing before the river, and ran unto him in the fury of his power.
>
> And I saw him come close unto the ram, and he was moved with choler against him, and smote the ram, and brake his two horns: and there was no power in the ram to stand before him, but he cast him down to the ground, and stamped upon him: and there was none that could deliver the ram out of his hand.
>
> Therefore the he goat waxed very great: and when he was strong, the great horn was broken; and for it came up four notable ones toward the four winds of heaven.

Piero della Francesco, *The Triumph of Chastity*
(fresco, Palazzo Uffizi, Florence)

And out of one of them came forth a little horn, which waxed exceeding great, toward the south, and toward the east, and
toward the pleasant land.

And it waxed great, even to the host of
heaven; and it cast down some of the host
and of the stars to the ground, and
stamped upon them.

Yea, he magnified himself even to the
prince of the host, and by him the daily
sacrifice was taken away, and the place of
his sanctuary was cast down.

And an host was given him against the
daily sacrifice by reason of transgression,
and it cast down the truth to the ground;
and it practised, and prospered. (8:3-13;
emphasis added)

Later in this chapter, Daniel seeks the meaning of
his vision, which is revealed by the angel Gabriel:

And his power shall be mighty, but not
by his own power: and he shall destroy
wonderfully, and shall prosper, and prac-
tise, and shall destroy the mighty and the
holy people.

And through his policy also he shall
cause craft to prosper in his hand; and he
shall magnify himself in his heart, and by
peace shall destroy many: he shall also
stand up against the Prince of princes; but
he shall be broken without hand. (8:24-25)

We may read this chapter in Daniel simply as an
allegorical apocalypse, where the vision of the ram,
the he-goat, the horns should be interpreted as ap-
plying to the historical events and kings. But the vision of the he-goat with one horn contains some interesting elements that later become the components
of the myth of the Unicorn as both the expected and
blessed savior, as well as the evil destroyer who

Hieronimus Bosch, *Garden of Delights*
(triptych, El Prado, Madrid)

fought even against the "Prince of princes," "cast down the sanctuary and the truth to the ground," prospered, became mighty but "not by his own power," "destroyed wonderfully," yet at the end "shall be broken without hand."

In the Book of Daniel we are not told what will happen to the transfigured he-goat after "he shall be broken without hand." What happened to the mighty horn the first time—broken into four, but growing anew as a mighty horn—could happen again. After all, the he-goat fulfilled a positive, sanctified mission, not only when he killed the ram but also when he destroyed "wonderfully" the mighty and the holy, by peace, or when he stood up against the Prince of princes, who is hard to identify: was it God (never called by this name in the Hebrew Bible) or was it the devil?

In any case, the vision of Daniel about the one-horned he-goat remains ambiguous, and it is open to different, contradictory interpretations. (A similar apocalyptic vision is repeated in the Book of Enoch, I.) St. Basil, in *Exegetic Homilies*, said that Christ "will be called the Son of Unicorns. For, as we have learned in Job, the Unicorn is a creature irresistible in might and unsubjected to man. . . ."[40]

But in one version of St. Basil's commentaries on the Psalms, we read:

> The Unicorn is evilly inclined toward man. It pursues him and when it catches him up it pierces him with its horn and devours him.
>
> Take care then, O Man, to protect thyself from the Unicorn, that is to say from the Devil. For he is ill-inclined toward man and skilled in doing him harm.[41]

According to St. Gregory the Great, in his *Moralia in Job*, the Unicorn is the "terrenus princeps" (earthly prince); Gregory elaborated a whole scenario about the evil Unicorn and his transcendence into the divine one. According to Gregory, Saul of Tarsus was compared to a Unicorn when he persecuted the Christians, but God succeeded in tethering this Unicorn to the manger, feeding it the fodder of Holy Scripture. Thus Saul was converted into Paul, and God placed his trust in the Unicorn.

Albertus Magnus wrote that the Unicorn is Christ, whose might, typified by its horn, is irresistible. But at the beginning it was the Jewish Unicorn and appeared wild and unruly and drove out Adam and Eve from the Garden of Eden. He was the one who brought on the Flood and punished the Sodomites for their sins, and so on. Thus, wrote Albertus Magnus, this Unicorn rampaged in heaven and earth, until "our glorious Virgin accepted it into her lap, where it entered her citadel, that is to say the womb of her chaste body . . . wherein in accordance with divine decree the unseizable creature might be captured . . . and yield voluntarily to death by crucifixion. . . ."[42]

The same idea or theme is repeated in the shrine altar to the Virgin Mary on the stairway of the Cologne Church of St. Mary (now in the Bonn Provincial Museum). Here too the Unicorn appears as a wild creature, attacking Adam, but the inscription says: "I am the Unicorn and a sign of God." The wild beast is tamed by the touch of the Virgin's fingers.

The meanings given in Christian literature to the diabolic nature of the Unicorn are various and related to the general context and purpose of the author. The Unicorn might, then, represent the devil, since he existed before the incarnation of Christ, antagonized him, or was connected to the first sin of Adam. Thus he is punished, on the one hand, but transcends to the divine Jesus on the other.

The allegories about the complex relations between Adam, Jesus, Devil, Unicorn, Eve, Mary, Gabriel served as appealing themes for many artists. Some of them even tried to include these themes in one tapestry, such as we see in the altar tapestry (c.1480) now in the Zurich Landesmuseum. The abundance of motifs and inscriptions in this tapestry is very confusing, and one has to rely on different histories of iconography and Christian theologians in order to get some coherence from them. (The tapestry even includes images from Daniel's vision.) But one theme is clearly expressed: the Unicorn here too is a wild, devilish creature who seeks his shelter and transcendence in Mary, who symbolizes the Church.

In other paintings, the Unicorn appears as the mighty devil, who can punish Adam and Eve and expel them from Paradise. Nicholas Cusanus goes even farther and says that the Unicorn *is* the God of the Old Testament, and it's not hard to see here the influence of a Gnostic concept, according to which the God of the Old Testament, or the Jewish God, is identified with the Demiurge or with Satan.

The same theme of the Unicorn as both divine and devil is repeated in many homilies, poems, paintings, and tapestries. Sometimes we find only the assessment, in words or pictures, that the Unicorn is the devil. Sometimes there is also some attempt to explain the reason why he is the devil. "And the vice of man's sin we may compare to the Unicorn," we read in a book of the late 15th century.[43]

Quite often the Unicorn seems to have been regarded as the devil because of his sexual desire, and only the Holy Virgin could transform him into a divine creature. But the devil Unicorn was not always saved by the Virgin and transfigured into Jesus. In an illustration to the Stuttgart psalter, we see the crucified Jesus attacked and stabbed by a wild Unicorn. In other illustrated psalters, Jesus—or some saint—is surrounded by wild animals, including the Unicorn, that look as if they are attacking him, but he apparently succeeds in taming them. Yet in other illustrations, the Unicorn is clearly drawn as the devil who sometimes lets a wild man—obviously a sinner—ride on his back.

All in all, there is much confusion in the concept of the Unicorn as devil or as a demonstration of devilish desires, intentions, and powers. Artists, poets,

Christ Attacked by a Unicorn (illustration, Stuttgart psalter, Württemberg Provincial Library, Stuttgart)

Mary, the Unicorn, Angels and Eve (tapestry, Landesmuseum, Zürich)

and even the wise theologians could not establish an unequivocal opinion about or image of the Unicorn: was he divine or diabolic, or both? One of the causes of this perpetual confusion was probably the interchange between the Christian concept and the ancient, pre-Christian myth of the erotic intercourse of the Unicorn and the maiden. Is the erotic desire per se good or evil, or both? Does the Unicorn present the divine nature of man or the diabolic one? The Unicorn has certainly suffered from the conflict in human nature and the self-perceptions projected upon him.

But after the Unicorn became a symbol of Jesus, the attitude toward the desirous creature captured by the maiden became much more complicated. The Church—especially in late Medieval times and during the Renaissance—emphasized the Incarnation of Jesus. The virgin capture, according to the *Physiologus* and its followers and interpretations, is an allegory of the Incarnation. The Unicorn represents Christ. The virgin is Mary. The huntsman is the Holy Spirit. Like the Unicorn, Jesus "agrees" to be captured, that is, to become a man, to die and to resurrect as a god.

But what was he *before* the Incarnation? Was he really willing to be captured and killed, therefore putting his head in the virgin's lap, or was he tempted by his wild desire and punished by the hunters? The obvious contradictions are related not only to the virgin—both holy and "she-devil"—as we see in many paintings, but also to the Unicorn himself: holy and sinner, fulfilling a divine mission and a symbol of the evil powers, savior and destroyer.

In a curious, usually not conscious way, the myth of the Unicorn demonstrates various and contradictory attitudes toward sex, toward the theological issues of Incarnation, toward the old questions of dualism and the relation between good and evil. I don't believe there is one theory that can explain the representations of the Unicorn as both divine and diabolic. I certainly don't believe that the poets, artists, theologians who wrote about the Unicorn or painted him had such a comprehensive theory. They were affected by many different associations, arguments, sources of inspiration. One can point out, for instance, as some scholars have done, the schism in the Church from the 11th century to the 13th or later concerning the problem of dualism and its relation to the Incarnation.[44] According to the official Roman Church, heaven and earth are a unity—a marriage affected by and symbolized in the Incarnation. When Christ became man, joining humanity and divinity in his own person, he healed the rupture created by the Fall; he humanized heaven and divinized the earth. According to the Catharists' doctrine—in a way continuing the traditions of the Gnostics and the Manicheans, whose sources may be found in the Zoroastrian religion and in the Mithraic cults—the cosmos was divided between the forces of good and evil, and the earth was entirely the province of Satan. Thus Christ and the Virgin Mary were spirits or angels, but not human beings, nor could they have been, since unity between God's dominion and Satan's was unthinkable. Since the myth of the Unicorn was associated with the myth of the Incarnation, it was affected by these problems of dualism, although in the artistic representations of this myth, these problems never were resolved, never found a clear, unequivocal answer.

One can also point out the importance of the courtly lore, as demonstrated in the poetry of the troubadours and minnesingers, where the woman is purity, joy, beauty that no man could reach or conquer and, also, the torturer, the one who always refuses to love. It is easy to see how the story of the Unicorn, captured by the woman, is related to this kind of poetry. Denis de Rougement argued that this poetic tradition grew out of the Catharist heresy.[45] True or not, many components of the Unicorn myth in poetry and painting can be related both to the Catharist doctrine about good and evil—or God and Satan—and the love poetry of the late medieval period. In both, the image of woman is regarded as damnation and salvation, "ce qui tente l'homme pour le perdre et ce que le sauve sur le plan de plus haut de l'esprit." (She is the one who tempts man in order to damn him, and she is the one who saves him on the highest spiritual level.)[46]

There is, then, an interesting parallel between the paintings of the Unicorn and the holy hunt and the persecution of the Catharists. They were the devils, hunted and persecuted by the Dominicans, who were called by the heretics "Domini Canes"—God's dogs. The Unicorn represents Catharism, and the Virgin represents the duplicitous Roman Church, a whore with a holy face. This interpretation certainly does not cover all the paintings of the Unicorn, or even the holy hunt, but it might have been one of the aspects of the Unicorn myth, or one of its sources. Again, we should not look for one comprehensive and unequivocal interpretation. The Unicorn in many poems and paintings could have been the suffering heretic or lover, and in others the sinner or the Devil himself. In the last analysis, he was both.

What we do know, what the medieval and Renaissance poets and artists knew, is that evil, or the devil, does exist, but must be conquered after bitter struggle, violence, and death. The Unicorn that we see or read about combines the two attitudes, often confused with each other: an approbation of the existence of the devil and a wish to conquer him or transfigure him into divinity.

The Unicorn as devil appears quite early. We can see him in a drawing from the 10th or 11th century, in the Duomo of Pisa, where two demonic Unicorns stand on either side of a woman holding a cross in her hand; in a 13th-century fresco, now partially effaced, in the Guild Chapel in Stratford-on-Avon, where a demonic Unicorn is guarding people tormented in hell; in a painting by Lucas Cranach the Elder (now in the Art Museum in Leipzig), where the Unicorn is either a one-horned monster or a devil; and in many other paintings, illustrations, reliefs, some of which

Lucas Cranach the Elder, *Des Sterbende* (painting, Künstmuseum, Leipzig)

I have yet to discover.

One of the best representations of the Unicorn as a devil is the etching by Dürer, *Abduction of Proserpine* (1516). Proserpine is riding on the back of Pluto-Unicorn, to hell. Erwin Panofsky says that the Unicorn—or at least this particular breed of him that appears in Dürer's etching—was associated with infernal regions, darkness, and night. In late medieval tradition, Pluto carries off his unwilling bride on horseback. Dürer developed the composition from his own drawing, in which an anonymous horseman dashes away with a naked woman. Dürer, according to Panofsky, eliminated the accessory figures, arranged the terrain so as to suggest a leap into the void, and transformed the horse into a fabulous Unicorn, evocative of the ideas of night, death, and destruction.[47]

It seems that for about 300 years (17th to 19th centuries) the myth of the Unicorn fell into serious decline, although it did not totally disappear from European literature and art. In the epoch of "rationalism" myths were regarded as superstitious obstacles on the road to progress, unworthy rivals to scientific thought. Still, the Unicorn itself attracted many men of science, even in that epoch. Odell Shepard mentions "rationalists" who wrote about the Unicorn in the 17th, 18th, and 19th centuries. Most of them, as far as I have learned, were still arguing the question of the Unicorn's existence.[48] Some of them were dealing mainly with the merits of the horn or debating the validity of proofs given by earlier writers. Coleridge, for instance, doubted the symbolism of the horn and wrote: "No one has yet discovered even a plausible origin for this symbolism as to horns."[49] I have read or rather browsed in only a few of these books, and my impression is that during this epoch, the myth of the Unicorn had lost its essence.

Still, the Unicorn did not die even then. He appeared in some works of romantic artists and poets.[50] He also remained alive in "primitive" folklore and in stories and rumors of travellers who claimed

Albrecht Dürer, *Abduction of Prosperine* (etching, Bettman Archive, New York)

to have seen him in remote parts of the world (Tibet, Southern Africa, Siberia, Ethiopia). He refused, so to speak, to perish. And when he did return to poetry and art, at the beginning of the 20th century, he reappeared in his previous character: savior and destroyer, divine and diabolic.[51]

In 1908, W.B. Yeats wrote his play *The Unicorn from the Stars*.[52] There we read that Martin Hearne painted a Unicorn and a lion on the coach he made. This ornament, or the flashing of light falling upon it, threw him into a trance, and he later told Father John:

> It was no dream, it was real. . . . There were . . . white horses rushing by . . . and we rode away, with the wind, like the wind. . . . We came to a sweet-smelling garden with a gate to it, and there were wheatfields in full ear around . . . and vineyards. . . . I thought it to be one of the townlands of Heaven. Then I saw the horses we were on had changed to Unicorns, and they began trampling the grapes. . . .
>
> *Father John.* That is strange. . . . What is it that brings to mind? I heard it in some place, *monoceros de astris*, the unicorn from the stars.
>
> *Martin.* . . . and I smelt the wine . . . then everything grew vague . . . we were all waiting for some command. . . . I was trying to hear it. . . . What was the command? Everything seemed to tremble around me. . . . It was terrible, wonderful! . . .
>
> *Father John.* I wonder what it all meant? The unicorns—strength they meant, virginal strength, a rushing, lasting, tireless strength. . . . It was a strange vision. . . .
>
> *Martin.* How can I get back to that place?
>
> *Father John.* You must not go back. . . .

That life of vision . . . is a terrible life, for
it has far more temptation in it than the
common life. . . . You cannot know but it
was from the Prince of this world the
vision came.

Martin. . . . I know that I saw the unicorns . . . and then a figure, a many-changing figure, holding some bright thing. I
know something was going to happen . . .
something that would make my whole life
strong and beautiful, like the rushing of
the unicorns . . .

. . . .

Johnny (letting bag fall with a crash).
Destruction on us all!

Martin: That is it! O, I remember. . . .
That is the command. . . . I saw a bright
many-changing figure; it was holding up a
shining vessel . . . then the vessel fell and
was broken with a great crash; then I saw
the Unicorns trampling it. They were
breaking the world to pieces . . . and I
shouted for joy. And I heard the command,
"Destroy, destroy, destruction is the life-
giver! destroy!" . . . They were breaking the
world. I am to destroy . . . to bring again
the old disturbed exalted life, the old
splendour . . .[53]

Later, Martin expresses his wish to extinguish the
Law and the Church, then "all life will become like a
flame of fire, a burning eye":[54]

Martin. We will go out against the
world and break it and unmake it . . . We
are the army of the Unicorn from the
Stars! . . . That is the joy of Heaven, con-
tinual battle. . . . I thought the battle was
here, and that the joy was to be found here
on earth, that all one had to do was to
bring again the old wild earth of the sto-

ries—but no, it is not here; we shall not
come to that joy, that battle, till we have
put out the senses . . . till we have brought
everything to nothing once again. . . . I saw
in a broken vision, but now all is clear to
me. Where there is nothing . . .—there is
God![55]

Yeats's vision is, of course, a personal one—the
symbolic vision of a poet at the beginning of the 20th
century—and should be read as such. But it does include several main elements that are typical of the
ancient and renewed myth of the Unicorn: the holy
paradisiac creature who can save the imaginary
world only by destroying the world—not only his enemy (the lion), but all the vanity of earth. Yeats certainly knew the vision of Daniel, and probably the
mystical writing of Konrad of Megenberg (1309-
1374) as well. In his *Book of Nature*, Konrad of
Megenberg wrote that Christ was the Unicorn because "before becoming man, he harbored wrath and
fury against the vanity of the angels and against the
stubbornness of the people of the earth."[56] If, then,
the Unicorn is to become the divine savior of the
world he must first be the destroyer and, in an am-
bivalent, mysterious way, Satan as well, the Prince
of Evil, enemy of Adam and of men.

In addition to the image of the Unicorn as the symbol, the representative or the emissary of the Devil,
he was often depicted as a symbol or emissary of
death. Here again, he is often ambiguous or double-
faced; namely, the Unicorn is life-giver and herald of
death, emissary of death and also of rebirth or resurrection. Sometimes these two contradictory roles
are separated and one of them is more explicit, more
emphasized than the other. Sometimes the Unicorn
plays the two roles simultaneously or is depicted in
an ambiguous way.

One of the earliest stories about the Unicorn as
symbol or emissary of death is an Indian fable from
the 6th century B.C.E., told by a wandering ascetic to

Buddha, thus teaching him about life and death. This story was translated into Arabic, Hebrew, Greek, in the 9th and 10th centuries C.E. and then into other European languages under the title *Barlaam and Josaphat* (both names were derived from Sanskrit: *bhagaran* and *bodhisat*). It was retold by Giacopo da Voragine, Archbishop of Geneva, in the 13th century and included in his *Legenda Aurea* (The Golden Legend):

> Once there was a man, Barlaam by name, who lived in the desert near Senaah and who often preached against the illusory pleasure of the world. Thus he spoke of a man fleeing in haste from a Unicorn who would drown him. Falling into an abyss or well he happened to catch hold of a bush but failed to find adequate foothold. With the raging Unicorn glaring down on him from the rim of the well, he caught sight of a dreadful fiery dragon waiting with open maw for him to drop. From the narrow ledge on which he was teetering, four serpents distended their fangs. A pair of mice, one black and the other white, gnawed away at the roots of the bush to which he was still clinging, while the bush itself was about to break off.
>
> But as he lifted his eyes, he spotted honey dripping from the branches of the bush, and forgetting all about his peril, he surrendered himself fully to the sweetness of the honey.[57]

The Unicorn, as Barlaam expounded in his parable, was death, which pursues man everywhere. The well was the world, filled with every evil. The bush was the Tree of Life—in an English translation, the bush bears an apple as well as the honey—always threatened by the constant erosion of the hours of night and day, represented by the black and white mice. The four serpents represented the human body, composed of the four elements. The dragon was the bottomless pit of hell, threatening to swallow up mankind. But the honey was worldly pleasure to which man surrenders, "forgetting all peril." (A nice illustration of this story is a copper engraving made by B. A. Bolswerth, 1580-1633, titled *The Man in the Well*, which is now in the University of Leyden.)

According to some interpretations of the story, the Unicorn's role is negative, since he represents death. But according to other versions and interpretations, the role of the Unicorn is positive: he was meant to teach man the "moral of life"—whatever it might be—by chasing him into the well or abyss, either to find there the Tree of Life or to forget the perils of death with the drops of honey he can find.[58] According to some versions and interpretations, the bush itself is the Tree of Life, and the Unicorn the one who, by chasing man into the well or abyss, leads him to this tree.

As in almost all the other motifs of the myth of the Unicorn, his role as an emissary of death—or even as a symbol of death—is ambiguous, a mixture of different and contradictory images and ideas. Thus we see him as a guardian of the dead, or of those doomed to die, in the relief on a sarcophagus in the museum of the cathedral in Ferrara, dating from the early 14th century. There he stands in a wheel, above him the script *Unicornis Iste Insequitru Animas Hominum* (The Unicorn Is The Guardian of Human Souls), and beneath him a crucified man surrounded by trees, and beneath that a fiery dragon's head.

In the church San Miniato del Monte in Florence (the Portuguese Chapel), a sarcophagus is supported by small angels. Beneath the sarcophagus are a wreath of flowers, a skull, and two guarding Unicorns. (The year of the death of Jacobus, who lies in the sarcophagus, is 1459.)

In a Gobelin from c. 1500 (now in the Musée Cluny, Paris), St. Stephanus's dead body is lying on a flowered ground, and he is guarded from above by angels. At his right side stands the Unicorn, probably guarding the dead against the lion, who appears in the same Gobelin.

More often the Unicorn's relationship to death is not so peaceful. When attacked by men, the Unicorn prefers to die rather than be caught. Thus he "springs up to the top of some precipice, whence he throws himself down and in the descent turns a somersault, so that the horn sustains all the shock of the fall."[59] John Guillim, in *A Display of Heraldry*, wrote about this subject:

> The greatness of the unicorn's mind is such that he rather chooseth to die than to be taken alive. . . . Wherein the unicorn and the valiant-minded soldier are alike . . . rather than they be compelled to undergo any base servitude or bondage, they will lose their lives.[60]

Another frequent story about the Unicorn's escaping his hunters is that while running away from them, or from the lion, he strikes his horn into a tree and there remains, whether dead or alive, no one can tell. In the Benedictine Abbey of Santa Maria in Praglia (near Padova), there is a sculpture of the Unicorn whose horn is stuck in a tree, presumably meant to represent the Tree of Life. The "act of suicide" is conceived as a symbolic act of the unity between death and life, or the expectation of rebirth or resurrection. In other words, although the Unicorn prefers death to captivity, his death is only a phase of transition to a new life.

The imagination of artists and poets created numberless variations of the stories about the peculiar relations between the Unicorn and death. Some of them might have been connected with the fearful image of the Unicorn and his erect, sharp horn. It seems as if he was created as a fierce beast, born in the unconscious fear of death and the need to conquer this fear, either by killing its cause or by capturing the animal and bringing him back to life in a different form. This is probably why some poets and artists related the Unicorn to Orpheus, the poet of rebirth or returning alive from the land of death. The same motivation, of conquering the fear of death by creating the Unicorn, was probably one of the main reasons for comparing the Unicorn with Jesus, the symbol of incarnation and resurrection.

In a tapestry from 1480 now in Zurich, which I've mentioned previously, Adam stabs the Unicorn and says: "But he is wounded because of our sins." Eve is collecting the blood of the Unicorn in a goblet and says: "And by his blood we are saved."

The same theme that identifies the Unicorn with Jesus, since both died in order to save men from death, is repeated in many religious poems from the late medieval period. But again, it is not necessarily a religious theme only. Many legends about the Unicorn have enriched his image as the creature who fulfills the double role and contains the opposite symbols of life and death.

In *The Lore of the Unicorn*, Shepard quotes a poem written by Natalis Comes (16th century) about the Unicorn that lived "on the edge of the world," that was "terrible unto his foe," and that, when the poisoners fouled the river by their secret poisons, would come and dip his horn in the water, "cleansing the venom away," so that "the forest-dwellers may drink once more." This beast, the poem tells us, "delights in the embrace of a virgin, falling asleep in her arms," but awakening, "he finds he is bound by ropes and by shackles."[61]

According to Shepard, "there is no suggestion [in this poem] of religious allegory, or of anything that would seem supernatural to the author."[62] Shepard may be right, and the poet really may have meant to tell a story about a "real" beast that was captured by his enemies. Yet the poem ends by saying:

Strange is the tale, indeed, yet so, they say, he

is taken,
Whether it be that the seeds of love have been
sown by great Nature
Deep in his blood, or for some more hidden
mysterious reason.[63]

In this poem, too, the Unicorn is mighty, stronger than all his enemies, and saves the "forest-dwellers from death," yet because of some "hidden mysterious reason," he is captured and taken (the poem doesn't say where, and we may only guess that he was taken to the land of death, but probably to resurrection too.)

The mystery, indeed, is innate in the creation of the myth, and his drama remains mysterious in all the legends about his death and his role as a saver of lives by purifying poisoned water, and his resurrection, whether perceived as a religious symbol or not.

In the *Basler Totentanz* (1440, of which there remains only a copy, now in the Art History Museum in Basel), Adam and Eve stand on one side of the Tree (of Knowledge? or of Life?) and on the other side three skeletons are dancing the Dance of Death. A lion stands nearby, close to the dancers. By the side of Adam and Eve, the Unicorn is crouching, watching them. Is he the devilish seducer or the natural companion of death, reproaching Adam and Eve for their sin? The interpretation of this sketch should probably still be religious.

In a Gobelin entitled *Allegorie de l'éphémère* (now in the Cleveland Museum of Art), we see on the left Youth, leading its happy carefree life, and, on the right, an old man being brutally cudgelled by a younger man. Near this cruel scene, a white Unicorn crouches as though quite uninterested. One must take the Unicorn here as a symbol of death. The whole Gobelin is not meant to be religious, but the mysterious role of the Unicorn is still there.

The myth of the Unicorn as representing death, or the awareness and fear of death, could be related directly to a certain Christian interpretation of the Fall

The Basler Totentanz (drawing, Historische Museum, Basel)

Allegorie de l'éphémère (tapestry, Cleveland)

of Adam, his expulsion from paradise, and his death. But the myth of the Unicorn might also derive from other, ancient sources or have been invented independently by artists and poets. In any case, we can combine the various stories and artistic representations of the Unicorn-death into a comprehensive and unified myth: the paradisiac Unicorn leaves paradise—whether expelled as a sinner and carrier of death or urged by desire and life-giving motivation. He fights for life; he is chased by devils or by holy hunters; he is seduced by a woman, is captured or dies, or exists in a hidden limbo between life and death. At the end of the story, he is resurrected and usually appears in a different, more benign and gentle form than his first appearances, inside paradise or outside, in some substitute for paradise.

In most of the stories and tapestries, we find only fragments of the Unicorn's myth as savior and destroyer, dead and resurrected. But in several works of art we can see these fragments combined into a whole panorama. One of them is *The Hunt of the Unicorn*, a set of six copper engravings made by Jean Duvet (1485-1556) now in the British Museum. The theme of the whole set is the triumph of love, and it was meant to honor the love of Henry II and Diane de Poitiers, for whom the Unicorn apparently had special relevance. (In the painting of her by Francis Clouet [1522-1572], now in the National Gallery, Washington, D.C., the Unicorn appears in a picture hanging in the background.) The fifth plate shows the Unicorn ridden by an amorino, and the sixth plate shows him in a triumphal procession, with an amorino about to crown him with a wreath of leaves. But the first four plates include some traditional elements of the Unicorn legend, such as the beginning of the hunt in the first plate, the Unicorn dipping his horn into a river in the second, fighting the hunters and goring one of them in the third, and tamed by a maiden and tied by the hunters in the fourth. In Jean Duvet's engravings the Unicorn is not holy or divine, but he still demonstrates the mystery of the creature who plays the role of emissary of both death and the lover's triumph.

The most conclusive panorama of this story about the hunt, death, and resurrection of the Unicorn can be found in the famous tapestries of the hunt, now in the Cloisters in New York City. As I said in Chapter 2, these tapestries should not be interpreted as a religious allegory; and, in my opinion, Margaret B. Freeman and John Williamson are exaggerating by imposing this kind of interpretation on each panel and each detail. But whatever the designers and artisans consciously intended to represent, there is no doubt that when the tapestries were made (in the beginning of the 16th century), the legends of the hunt, the death and resurrection of the Unicorn were known, and they can easily be associated with each of the panels. In any case, many of the scenes depicted evoke the familiar legends.

Thus we may associate the beginning of the hunt in the first panel with the traditional story about the holy hunt, and even detect in the fourth panel the figure of the archangel Gabriel as one of the hunters.[64] In the second panel, the Unicorn is dipping his horn in the fountain. No matter, then, what the artist (or artisan) meant to show, the association of this scene with a whole body of allegories about the meaning of the horn/cross dipped in the water can also be easily evoked. In the third and fourth panels, the Unicorn is trying to escape from the hunters, then is fighting for his life, but his fate is already sealed. In the fifth panel, he is tamed by a maiden whose face and gesture are rather dubious, if not mischievous. She certainly doesn't represent the Virgin, but her role in the hunt may evoke the known stories about the maiden, especially since she stands inside an enclosed garden. In the sixth panel, the Unicorn is killed by the hunters, and then—in the same panel—he is carried to the king's palace. In this panel, the king himself and his whole entourage are quite secular, but the mere connection between the death of the Unicorn and the king's palace is sufficient to

The Unicorn at the Fountain (tapestry, The Cloisters, New York)

The Unicorn in Captivity (tapestry, The Cloisters, New York)

evoke the associations of the traditional legend of the holy hunt.

In the seventh panel, we see the Unicorn in captivity—one of the most famous images, I believe, of the Unicorn until our time.[65] His figure, size, gesture are quite different from those of the Unicorn in the other panels. It might even be that he was made by a different artist, who wished to end the story of the hunt in a conciliatory way. Nevertheless, the Unicorn-in-captivity can be perceived as an image of resurrection, inside the enclosed garden and surrounded by the holy tree and flowers. He is chained to a pomegranate tree by a collar of love. I don't know if the Unicorn in this panel is "meant to represent the risen Christ as well as the fertile Adonis," as one of the experts on the Cloisters tapestries has written.[66] But he certainly opens the gate to this kind of interpretation or to similar ones associating him with many other legends about the death and resurrection of the Unicorn.

Yet, even if we accept the tradition of the stories shown in the Cloisters tapestries, the myth of the Unicorn is still not exhausted by them. They still leave us with many unresolved questions, and with the need to continue our search.

1. Einhorn, 112-118 deals with this motif of the Unicorn and paradise; 389-392 lists illustrated Bibles.

2. One of the nicest examples I've seen is the series of copper etchings by Andrea Pizani, now in the Museo del Duomo, Florence.

3. Saint Basil, *Exegetic Homilies*, 204-205. About the diabolic nature of the Unicorn, see Einhorn, 56-58, 115-118.

4. Talmud, Chulin, 60a.

5. Talmud, Sabath, 26b.

6. Ettinghausen, *The Unicorn*, 62-63.

7. Arthur Boyd and Peter Porter, *The Lady and the Unicorn* (London: Sacker, 1975) 9.

8. Julius Solinus, *Polyhistoria*, trans. Arthur Golding in *The Excellent and Pleasant Works of Julius Solinus Polyhistor* (Gainsville, Florida: Scholars Reprints, 1955) 198.

9. Quoted from Bartholomeus Angelicus, *De Propiertatibus Rerum* XVIII, trans. John of Trevias (Westminster, 1494) 90. This passage follows Isidor's *Origines*, which was one of the most popular bestiaries in the Middle Ages.

10. Quoted in Ettinghausen, 35.

11. Ettinghausen, 60.

12. Ettinghausen, 64-65.

13. Shepard, 216.

14. Einhorn, 154. My translation.

16. Ettinghausen, 66.

16. Gustave Flaubert, *The Temptation of Saint Antony*, trans. Killy Mrosovsky (New York: Penguin, 1980) 88-89, 230. Flaubert probably knew Lamprecht's 12th-century *Alexanderlied*, which tells a similar story.

17. For instance, see John Swan, *Speculum Mundi* (Cambridge, 1635) 435; MacEanly, *History of England* (London, 1849) 430*ff.* This list of books dealing with the merits of the horn is quite long, and some scholars (Shepard, Beer, Einhorn, Ettinghausen) have written whole chapters on this subject. I've read only a few of the books mentioned by these scholars. In many of them, though, the merits of the horn are discussed without a direct connection to the myth of the Unicorn himself. Many of the authors of these books were physicians or alchemists, preoccupied by the need to prove the medical or merchandisable value of the horn and less interested in the myth of the Unicorn.

18. *Parzifal*, 482, 24; 483, 1; 232. My translation.

19. Emil Peters, *Physiologus* (Munich: 1971) 34-35. My translation. Also see St. Basil, Homily 13, 207-208.

20. Quoted in Shepard, 214.

21. Fray Luis de Orreta, *Historia de los Grandes y Remotos Reynos de la Etiopia, Monarchia del Emperador llamado Preste Juan* (Valencia, 1610); quoted in Shepard, 67.

22. Ettinghausen, 105. The origin of the story about Rsyasrnga, who cursed the gods and stopped the rains, is told by O'Flaherty in *Siva*, 45.

23. *Ikkaku Sennin* (The One-Horned Rishi), a summary of the 15th-century No play in Arthur Waley, *The No Plays of Japan* (New York: Grove, 1957) 288-289.

24. Guillaume le Clerc, *Bestiaire Divin* in *Bestiaires du Moyen Age*, ed. Gariel Bianciotto (Paris: Stock, 1980) 92.

25. Thomas Wright, *Popular Treatises on Science Written in the Middle Ages* (London: 1596; York: Scholar, 1970) 75.

26. Quoted in Freeman, 68.

27. Freeman, 68.

29. *Midrash Schocer Tor*, Chapter 22.

30. See, for example, C.G. Jung, *Psychology and Alchemy*, *Collected Works* 12 (New York: Pantheon, 1953.)

31. Robert Brown, *The Unicorn: A Mythological Investigation* (London: 1871) 86.

32. Alexander Porteous, *Forest Folklore, Mythology and Romance* (London: Allen, 1928) 191-202.

33. Edmund Spenser, *The Works of Edmund Spenser*, ed. Edwin Greenlaw et al. (Baltimore, Md.: Johns Hopkins UP, 1933) *The Faerie Queene*, 2. 5. 10.

34. Topsell, 91.

35. *La Romance de la Dame à la Lycorne et du Biau Chevalier du Lion* (Dresden: Geselschaft für romantische Literatur, 1908) 166-173.

36. See Beer, 121.

37. See Alain Erlande-Brandenburg, *The Lady and the Unicorn* (Paris: Réunion des Musées Nationaux, 1985) 10-14, 6-78.

38. See the introduction and the study by Erlande-Brandenburg in *The Lady and the Unicorn*, 10-14, 65-78. George Sand had written about these tapestries in her novel *Jeanne* (1844) as well as in several essays.

39. See Einhorn, 330.

40. St. Basil, "Homily on Psalm 28," *Exegetic Homilies*, trans. Sister Agnes Clare Way (Washington, DC: Catholic UP, 1963) 204-205.

41. Pseudo-St. Basil, quoted in Beer, 97.

42. Albertus Magnus, *De animalibus libri* XXVI, trans. J. Scanlan (New York: Binghamton, 1987), 180-181.

43. Bartholomes di Libri, *Fior di virtù* (Florence, 1491); quoted by Einhorn, 98.

44. See Lidico Mohacsy, "The Legend of the Unicorn," *Journal of the American Academy of Psychoanalysis* 12:3, 1984, 387-412. Dr. Mohacsy has elaborated this thesis in his paper "The Medieval Unicorn: Historical and Iconographic Application of Psychoanalysis," presented at the meeting of the American Academy of Psychoanalysis in New York, January 1987. In this paper, Dr. Mohacsy gives a sophisticated interpretation of the conjuncture of Melanie Klein's theory of ambiguity in child/mother relations and the history of Catharism. His information was valuable for me; not so his speculations.

45. Denis de Rougemont, *Love in the Western World*,

trans. M. Belgion (New York: Harper, 1974).

46. D. Roché, *Le Catharisme* (Toulouse: Institut d'Etudes Occitanes, 1947), quoted in Mohacsy, 34.

47. Erwin Panofsky, *Albrecht Dürer* II (Princeton, NJ: Princeton UP, 1964), 196.

48. See Shepard, 177-190.

49. S.T. Coleridge, *Literary Remains* I, *The Complete Works of Coleridge* V (New York: Harper, 1884) 120.

50. For example, in Keats's *Endymion*, E.T.A. Hoffman's *Prinzessin Brambilla*, A. von Arnim's *Die Kronenwächtet*, Böcklin's painting *The Isle of the Dead*, and there must be other works that I've not read or seen.

51. In *Spiritalis Unicornis* (270-272), Einhorn gives a long list of 20th-century writers and painters in whose works the Unicorn appears, figuratively or symbolically.

52. W. B. Yeats, *The Unicorn from the Stars, Collected Plays* (London: Macmillan, 1960) 327-383. I quote only the passages that refer directly to the Unicorn and evade the intention and meaning of the play.

53. Yeats, *Unicorn*, 337-339, 343-346.

54. Yeats, *Unicorn*, 360.

55. Yeats, *Unicorn*, 381-382.

56. Quoted in Beer, 50

57. Quoted in Beer, 52.

58. Einhorn, 219-224, cites a long list of versions of the story of Barlaam and Josaphat in several languages.

59. Quoted by Ettinghausen, 93. Ettinghausen mentions some Arabic versions of the story in the Manafi (1297?) but it is not clear whether they refer to the Unicorn, the rhinoceros, or the Persian wild goat.

60. John Guillim, *A Display of Heraldry* (London: Hall, 1611), section III, chapter 4. No numeration.

61. Quoted in Shepard, *Lore*, 61.

62. Shepard, *Lore*, 282, n38.

63. Shepard, *Lore*, 61.

64. See Freeman, *The Unicorn Tapestries* and Williamson, *The Oak King*.

65. At least two writers devoted books to a theme based on this image of the Unicorn: Stanley Stewart, *The Enclosed Garden* (Madison: U of Wisconsin P, 1966) and Lotte K. Hahn, *The Unicorn Who Wanted To Be Seen* (New York, Oxford UP, 1961).

66. Williamson, *The Oak King*, 226.

The Unicorn, the Maiden, and a Hunter (enameled silver tray, Nationalmuseum, Munich)

In Quest of the Unicorn

> *He had felt jostled and lonely at the border of his constellation, only a little town shivering in tempered space.*
>
> *To the questioner: "Have you finally met her? Are you happy at last?" he did not deign to reply, and tore a leaf of guelder rose.[1]*

I began my quest for the Unicorn after looking at Paul Rotterdam's drawings. The Unicorn himself does not appear in these drawings. He remains a secret, a hidden mystery, encompassed and concealed. What we can see there is only an opening to the mystery, the gateway to a myth that bursts out of unknown depths and might be the focus of absolute love or unity of emotions but might also be the gateway of anxiety, of fear to face the threat of annihilation, of nothingness, which is at the same time the gateway to the beyond. The Unicorn himself must remain a mystery, an enigma.

Ambrose Paré, who lived in the 17th century, said that the Unicorn must have been feigned by painters and writers. Rilke, in his *Sonnets to Orpheus*, wrote that artists and poets loved the Unicorn, and thus the creature that never was "came to be. They always left space enough . . . for the possibility that it might be. And they gave the animal so much power. . . ."[2] It is his power to be seen, though he never was seen; to be alive, though he died so many times; to be free, though he was captured and probably killed. The Unicorn tempts artists and poets to capture him; he still desires to be seen, yet never reveals who and what he is or where he lives.

The hidden Unicorn of Rotterdam's drawings continues an old tradition, renewed time and again in our era, of a quest that is never resolved, of a creature that remains unknown. It seems that from the earliest stories of the Unicorn—verbal and visual—up until the 20th century, the imaginary creature has refused to reveal his secret lest the revealing would be the destruction of its essential entity as a mysterious vision. Any concrete physical representation might threaten to block the way to the surreality of the hidden enclosure, the only place where the Unicorn can exist. The Unicorn in René Char's poem "The Ring of the Unicorn" does not answer the questions posed to him, since any attempt to answer them will ruin the essence of his mysterious existence. The Father in Yeats's play warns Martin not to watch the "terrible, wonderful" vision of the Unicorns, since it might end with destruction and death. At the end of this play, Father John says "He [Martin] is gone and we can never know where that vision came from." Since its earliest beginnings, the myth of the Unicorn has been bound up with pain, with the confrontation between the dream of Eden—an isolated, mysterious island of some absolute unity with love, with God—and the tormenting knowledge that Eden cannot be reached. The Unicorn himself cannot be revealed in this vision, nor does the artist who paints him or writes about him know who the Unicorn is.

In my search for the Unicorn, I have found many works of art where the maiden, or lady, is holding a mirror in front of the Unicorn as if intending to show him his identity. In *The Notebooks of Malte Laurids Brigge*, Rilke describes one of the panels of *La dame à la licorne* in the Musée Cluny:

> She curves her other arm toward the unicorn, and the creature bridles, flattered, and rears and leans upon her lap. It is a mirror, the thing she holds. See: she is showing the Unicorn its image. . . .[3]

And in the sonnet to Orpheus that I have already mentioned in the Prologue, Rilke refers to the same panel:

> *To a maiden he came thereby, all white—*
> *and was inside the mirror-silver, and in her.*

But actually the Unicorn did not see his full image in that mirror, only a part of it, and only a part of his horn. Amazingly, in almost all the mirrors that face the Unicorn, we don't see his image. The mirror was presented in some paintings and engravings as a tool to help the hunters capture the Unicorn. We can see it, for instance, on a French ivory casket from the 14th century (now in the Metropolitan Museum of Art in New York): the maiden or lady is holding the mirror and the horn, while the Unicorn is being stabbed by a hunter—but again, the mirror is blank. In a miniature by Mâitre François, c. 1470, in the Wharmcliffe Book of Hours, the lady is holding a mirror in front of a Unicorn, but he turns his head away, as if not daring to look at his reflection. On a *marmor intarsia* from the 16th century in the Catherine Chapel in Siena, Adam (some scholars say it is not Adam but Orpheus) is sitting beneath a tree in paradise, holding a mirror to show the Unicorn his reflection, but the Unicorn cannot see it there; the mirror is blank.

I have read several interpretations of the use of the mirror confronting the Unicorn. One of them says that the mirror is the symbol of the Immaculate Virgin, but since the mirror is present in some scenes without the maiden, there must also be other reasons for its relationship to the Unicorn. So far as I know, the Unicorn is the only mythical creature that is incited to look at himself in the mirror, yet cannot or doesn't see there his reflection.

(One other mythical creature that looked at his reflection in some kind of mirror—actually a pool of water—was Narcissus. Rilke mentions him in the Third Sonnet to Orpheus as analogous to the Unicorn. This analogy between Narcissus and the Unicorn was made several times before Rilke—by Bernart de Ventaton, Rhinrich von Morengen, Jacob Böhme, and others.[4] But we know that when Narcissus looked at his reflection in the water, he committed suicide. The Unicorn was probably stabbed with the help of the mirror, but remained alive, or resurrected.)

Mirrors, then, were used by artists in order to capture the Unicorn, but in the final account they failed. The reason for this failure may be attributed to the mirrors, as Rilke has written:

> *Mirrors: no one's ever yet described*
> *you, knowing what you really are.*
> *Time's interstices, you seemed filled with*
> *nothing but the holes of filters.*
> . . . .
> *At times, you're full of painting. A few*
> *seem to have seeped into you—*
> *others you shyly sent away. . . .*[5]

But it may be that mirrors cannot catch the image of the Unicorn because he is too mysterious, too ambiguous, and must remain so. All that artists and painters can do is search for the gate to his hidden and enigmatic kingdom. The mirror, then, accentuates the enigmatic character of the Unicorn. Poets and artists have always been attracted by myths and mythical creatures. In fact, whatever we know now about myths is, in most cases, due to works of art and poetry, long after the original myths have disappeared and died, together with the specific cultures that begot them. When poets and artists in modern times are attracted by a myth, they can revive only the memories of a "lost paradise." They can and do apply different interpretations to each myth, change it, add to it their own speculations and imagination. The stories about each mythical hero—god, demigod, human, animal—may have many variations or metamorphoses, depending on the variety of cultures in which they are born or on the different inclinations of the poet, the artist, the scholar. All of the myths evade any final comprehensive definition. Yet each one of them is based on a complete story and reveals the function and the fate of each of its participants.

The story of the Unicorn, however, in all its manifestations, differs from all other myths. The Unicorn

Magdalena Abakanowicz, *A Head of a Unicorn*
(sculpture, courtesy Marlborough Gallery,
New York)

himself does not fit into any of the categories that apply to the participants of any other myth known to us or revived in post-mortem art and poetry. Actually, we don't have one Unicorn story at all, but a dispersed and random variety of stories, poems, religious homilies, treatises, paintings, tapestries, engravings, statues. The hero of them all is a strange, mysterious creature who cannot be described or defined by his function or character. He is always represented in diversified forms and contexts. He always plays multifarious roles, serves different and contradictory purposes, functions as a subject of heterogeneous stories, visions, allegories. In most, if not all, of his representations, he is not confined to any consistent and specific connotation. His various images are always the juxtaposition of a "natural" creature and a symbolic or transcendental one. He is always endowed with the unique gift of being simultaneously a secular and a religious symbol, real and metaphorical, exposed and hidden. He signifies strength and weakness, vanity and humility, desire and chastity, good and evil, life and death.

Look, for instance, at the physical shape of the Unicorn as he is described in separate stories, or even in the same story: always a combination of a living animal—a rhinoceros, a wild ass, a horse, a kid, a human animal—and a non-existent or supernatural and surrealistic one. He may appear as a kid with elephant feet, a horse with a horn simulating a flute, a horse with a goat's beard, a man with a horn between his eyes. In all these combinations we can detect a tendency to represent the vicissitudes and contradictions that characterize human nature, together with an unconscious need to project that nature on some *other* creature, both similar to the human and separate from it.

We can say, of course, that all mythical creatures are in their own way projections of the human psyche. But in most of the myths, the creatures born of this projection acquire their separate, "independent" modes of existence. Not so the Unicorn. He never acquired total independence and separation. He has always remained in a no-man's land between the act of the inventing imagination and the need to implant the imaginary creature in the body of a natural, "objective" entity. While other myths conceal the elements of human projection and attribute to their heroes their separate modes of existence, as it were, the myth or myths of the Unicorn reveal these elements, although in ambiguous ways, revealing and concealing simultaneously, in the same creature, the same story. The Unicorn—even in the story of Indian Rsyasrnga—was never identified directly with a "natural" human creature. Every representation of the Unicorn as human or analogous to human seems also to emphasize a difference. No less than resembling a human being—by straight analogy, by allegory, by allusions to similar fate—the Unicorn represents the projection of a need and desire to become *other* than simply human, to be detached from human, earthly life. All the unicorns, throughout the history of their stories, yield to their human fates, yet are also capable of transcending themselves and conquering their weaknesses and evil inclinations, conquering death, too, though not before they go along the *via dolorosa* toward death.

I don't believe we can trace the original source of the myth of the Unicorn. It may have been derived from several different sources: the Indian story about the human-Unicorn, and the legends about a strange, one-horned animal living in some exotic unknown place. Later medieval versions of this myth could have been a combination of these different sources, together with the inclination of medieval artists and scholars toward allegory, for which the Unicorn was most suitable. In any case, the Unicorn was found or invented as the most suitable creature both to represent human nature and to project it on another creature. This combination of human and trans-human is the genuine myth of the Unicorn, and also the mystery of it.

(We know, of course, about similar combinations

of the natural and the supernatural, the human and the transhuman, in the images of the centaur, the nymph, the siren, the cyclops, and other mythical creatures.[6] But they were rather short-lived. They have disappeared with the culture that begot them and have reappeared only seldom in some works of art and poetry in later times. Few modern artists have invented their own mythical creatures that combine the human or "natural" with the surrealistic. The Unicorn has maintained this combination through many centuries and different cultures and works of art.)

This unique characteristic of the myth has enabled artists and poets to attribute to the Unicorn the antagonistic connotations of his form, his behavior, his nature. Look, for example, at the horn, the most distinct mark of the Unicorn. Was it borrowed from nature? There are many speculations about the probability that the Unicorn's horn was created due to some error in perspective; i.e., that some artist or eyewitness saw the horns of an oryx or antelope in profile and thought he saw only one horn of an existing animal. Other speculations say that the Unicorn's horn was an artistic imitation of the narwhal's horn or the horn of the rhinoceros.[7] Whether real or not, the Unicorn's horn became independent of its alleged origin. In all cases, it had the flexibility to become supernatural, surrealistic, symbolic. It was always loaded with different or contradictory connotations: the same horn, quite often in the same story or painting, signified the phallus, sexual desire, and was also the symbol of chastity and humility. The same horn could represent the might of God or the longing for unity with God, and also was the symbol of vanity, ferocity, animosity to men and God. One might wonder how the same artist, or even the same theologian, could attribute to the horn such opposing characteristics. They may have been unaware of the contradictory elements in their poems, paintings, homilies. But they could accept them, express them, since they were dealing with the mystery of human nature, its vicissitudes and conflicts. They borrowed the Unicorn, or reinvented him, as the most suitable paradigm of this mystery.

The same could be said about the hunt of the Unicorn. Whatever the sources of the scenes of the hunt—realistic or legendary, antique or contemporary—the Unicorn in these scenes and stories always reveals his unique and antagonistic behavior. He is simultaneously trying to rescue himself, to fight against the hunters and their hounds, to escape his fate, and also yielding willingly, seeking shelter in the bosom of a woman—lover or mother—or in the king's palace. The hunters, too, are both the enemies of the Unicorn and emissaries of love or of God, intending to kill the Unicorn yet ready to save him and to bring him to the bosom of a woman or to the king's palace. They are always both realistic and allegorical hunters.

The same is true, as we have seen, about the woman and her role in the hunt: temptress and chaste maiden, lover and emissary of death, an agent of sin and of a divine goal. The background of the hunting scenes—the trees, the palace, the enclosed garden—are always loaded with different and mysterious connotations. They allude both to a natural, realistic scene of the hunt and to a secluded enclave of paradisiac love or to a symbolic divine place. In some aspects of the hunt and the behavior of the Unicorn while chased by hunters, we can detect the famous conflict between eros and thanatos. A modern poet referred to it when he wrote, "Kannst du, mein Tod, nicht kommen als Einhorn." (Can't you, my death, come as a Unicorn.)[8]

But even the stories and scenes of the hunt, as well as other tales, allude to a broader complex of motives: the Unicorn must be killed in order to be reincarnated as a divine, everlasting being. The motif of death and resurrection is central in many myths. Mythical heroes and gods do die and return to life. The myths of Adonis, Osiris, Dionysus, Tamuz are certainly common myths and the foundation of many legends, rituals, and religions. The myth of the Unicorn was probably influenced and inspired by them and assimilated by many of their components.[9] Yet it differs from them, since it always reveals, directly or indirectly, its human aspects. Hence the analogy between the Unicorn and the myth of Jesus, certainly one of the most human myths of the death and resurrection of God.

During the Middle Ages and the early Renaissance, the allegory of the Unicorn as Jesus and of the maiden as Mary was one of the central motifs in all the stories and paintings of the Unicorn. It appeared, as we have seen, in many homilies, in illustrations of psalters, in engravings made for churches and in tapestries. But even the stories that were directly related to Jesus and Mary included other elements, which do not correlate the Unicorn with this allegory. How could Jesus be sexually tempted by his virgin mother? How could he desire her as a lover? The allegory of the Unicorn as Jesus could develop only by becoming a new myth, one that assimilated other motifs and was inspired by other motivations. Some of them were probably borrowed from earlier myths, but some of them were the fruits of a creative imagination that attributed to the Unicorn other traits, begotten by the projection of human conflicts, the conjunction of eros and thanatos, the ideal of chivalric love, and the quest for transcendence, for redemption through reincarnation, for the return to the lost paradise.

Thus the myth of the Unicorn could retain the allegorical elements of Jesus and Mary, of the incarnation of God in a human body and his reincarnation, and also include them in a more complex myth that represents the human concept of itself, its hopes and fears, strength and weakness, good and evil, by projecting them onto a mythical creature and at the same time transcending them.

In the last account, the quest for the Unicorn is the repeated quest for a myth that will combine opposites—the real and the surreal, the natural and the supernatural, the earthly and the divine—in one creature, one story, one work of art. In spite of the differences between one Unicorn and another, there is one common element in all the poems, stories, paintings in which the Unicorn is represented: he is always a being that wants to be captured and seen, yet at the same time wants to return to his mysterious enclosure, to be hidden there and remain unseen. He is always the subject of this continuing longing and quest.

Artists and poets did not feign the Unicorn. They created the original, unique myth of an enigmatic, mysterious creature who tends to die and be resurrected, hide and reveal himself, from antique times until now.

1. René Char, "The Ring of the Unicorn," trans. Mary Ann Caws, in *The Poems of René Char*, trans. Mary Ann Caws and J. Griffin (Princeton, NJ: Princeton UP, 1976), 275.

2. R.M. Rilke, *Die Sonnete an Orpheus*, II, 4; my translation.

3. Rilke, *Notebooks*, 113.

4. For the analogy between Narcissus and the Unicorn, see Einhorn, 178-179.

5. R.M. Rilke, *Sonnets to Orpheus*, Second Series, 3. Trans. A. Poulin, Jr. (Boston: Houghton Mifflin, 1977) 143.

6. Jorge Luis Borges told some interesting stories about such mythical creatures in *The Book of Imaginary Beings*. Also see Charles Gould, *Mythical Monsters* (London, 1886); Paul and Arin Johnsgard, *Dragons and Unicorns: A Natural History* (New York: St. Martin's, 1982); Florence McCulloch, *Medieval Latin and French Bestiaries* (Chapel Hill: NC UP, 1960); T.H. White, *The Book of Beasts* (New York: Dover, 1984).

7. Ettinghausen (Unicorn, 62*ff.*) quotes many examples from Arabian and Persian literature about the variety of animals—including the lion, the fox, the snake—that served as "models" for the descriptions of the Unicorn. For the connection of the Unicorn and the narwhal, see Shepard, 253-272.

8. Wolfdietrich Schnurre, quoted by Beer, 208.

9. Williamson wrote about the motif of the dying god as a common element in the myth of Adonis and the myth of the Unicorn. *The Oak King*, 66-67, 102, 224-226.

Post Scriptum

Rereading my essay about the Unicorn, I feel I have not rendered him the justice he deserves. I've related a partial history of his myth. I've speculated about sources of his various appearances and the motivations of the artists and poets who created him and then, trying to pin down the essence of the mysterious animal, wrote about him, painted him, wove him into their tapestries, molded him in their sculptures and reliefs. Yet, after several years of being engrossed by both the myth and the story of the Unicorn, I feel I have not succeeded in capturing either of them. The mysteries remain as mysterious as they were in my first encounters with the Unicorn.

In most of the written stories about the Unicorn, as well as in many tapestries, frescoes, and reliefs, the animal is initially inclined to be hidden, invisible, unknown, and then to burst out—either because he is sexually tempted or because he is urged by inexplicable desire to be visible. Thus he is hunted, caught, sometimes killed. In the aftermath, the Unicorn is resurrected or returned to his hiding place, then reappears in a transformed shape. The same is true about the *myth* of the Unicorn. It started in an unknown hiding place, then came to life and became visible and concrete, then disappeared and reappeared again, transformed into stories, poems, paintings.

The poets and artists who created this myth, who turned the invisible into the visible, were fascinated by their own creation, regarding their creature with wonder and awe. Many of them tried to overcome their astonishment by attributing to their Unicorn the traits of a symbolic creature, to present him as an allegory, to interpret him as an incarnation of a divine force or a representation of some human qualities, both virtues and vices. But it is still difficult to answer the question of how and why both this enigmatic creature and persistent myth were born and kept alive through thousands of years and countless transformations. Why, and to what purpose, did all those who created the myth need the unique, one-horned creature in order to realize their imaginations?

During my search for the Unicorn, I was inclined to perceive him as the symbolization of an inner struggle between the subconscious human fear of potential forces that wish to remain hidden and the need to expose them in order to conquer them, to beautify them. To accomplish this dueling aspiration, the imaginative artists and poets projected their emotions and inner conflicts onto an "objective" creature, turned the inconceivable and invisible image into a concrete and visible being.

Many myths make no distinction between the "image"and the "object," between representation and real identity. They are related to certain rites that do not *represent* but are absolutely real. However, it seems to me that the significance and depth of the Unicorn myths lie not in what their configurations *reveal* but in what they *conceal*: a secret meaning, which can be glimpsed behind the images. The Unicorn has never had any rites nor any clear purpose.

It may be, then, that from its earliest appearance, the Unicorn's secret meaning was, and is, the power of representing an image or, rather, the power of the human imagination to create an image that through its own specific existence and behavior is meant to conceal its symbolic interpretation. However, in saying this, I'm afraid I have only elaborated another theory, another speculation, about the symbolic Unicorn. He still remains an arcanum, a myth more complicated than any theory can interpret.

Artists and poets created the Unicorn out of love. They did not need him for any practical purpose, not even a magical one. The Unicorn is probably the most abstract creature there is, a pure product of art. But they were also frightened of him and even killed him. Thus he eludes all attempts at rationalization, at theories. He simply exists: a work of art without any cause, any purpose.

It may be, then, that the best way to respond to the Unicorn myth is simply to look at the Unicorn as he appears in paintings and sculptures (some illustrations of which I present in my essay), and read the stories and poems related to him (some of which I've mentioned and quoted here). But all the artworks and poems cannot solve the enigma of this creature or decipher the puzzling motivations that caused artists and poets to create him and revive his story time and again. The most they can do is stimulate our curiosity to look at the Unicorn or read about him, and then stimulate our wonder and awe.

The Unicorn I've seen and written about is no longer a youthful creature overcome by desire, leaping over fences in order to reach a tempting maiden. The Unicorn I've seen is old, submissive, his horn bent. At the beginning of his saga he trampled the fields in joyful vigor, trod the stars under his hooves, fought hunters and purged the fountain from snakes' poison until he reached the maiden who was expecting him, bent his head, concealed his erect horn inside her skirt, relaxed, and fell asleep. Then he was captured and imprisoned in an enclosed garden, near a sealed fountain. There he grew old and lost the power to burst out of his prison and reach his beloved maiden. And she too grew old and did not try to seduce him. But she still expected him to come, not knowing if he would.

But then Orpheus arrived and began to play on his flute. All the other animals of paradise disappeared; the Unicorn alone was left to listen to the flute of Orpheus, along with the maiden, who was holding a mirror in her hand. Slowly the Unicorn raised his head to the sound of the music until he saw his reflection in the mirror, but he could not tell if he was a living creature or a dead and resurrected one, or if he had never existed at all except in a legend. But, to the sound of the music, the maiden approached him slowly, threw away the mirror, and held his horn until it re-erected. And the Unicorn concealed it in the folds of her skirt. And both of them listened to the sound of Orpheus's music.

I, of course, did not invent this story, nor did I see it in a dream. After following the Unicorn for many years, I just looked at him as if he were alive and concrete, filling my heart with wonder and awe.

M.M.
New York
March 1992

AB2-6822

11.2